The
Billie Shepard
Presentation Method

Why an acting teacher holds the key to
greater influence, happier customers,
and better relationships

Billie Shepard

Book layout by Rachel Hegarty
Cover design by Amier WildEagles99
Names: Shepard, Billie

Title: The Billie Shepard Presentation Method / by Billie Shepard

Description: 1st ed. | Mountain View, CA [2020] | Includes index.
ISBN 978-1-7345329-0-6 (paperback)
ISBN 978-1-7345329-1-3 (e-book)

Printed in the United States of America

Table of Contents

to my students

Appreciation

Thank you to all the business leaders who have recognized the value of this training and entrusted their employees, clients, and often themselves to my care.

Individual thanks to Lori Ciano, Wesley Jess, Aaron Sullivan, Natalie King, Bernard C. Coleman III, Lynne Born, Murray Cook, Rebecca Duffy, Jenny Cook, Laurie Hastings, Leslie Trigg, Delphine Bernard, Kim Pham, Sonia Nijhawan Mehra, Jeanmarie Guenot, Jim Shahbazian, Mayrose Munar, Wendy Taylor, Linda Nellis, Marianne Adoradio, and Rick Eigenbrod.

Thanks to Alan Arkin, Michael Kostroff, Judy Kaye, Mary Mackey, Mindi White, Adam Rosen, Debbie Olson, Heidi Mason, Nicky Ruxton, Rachel Hegarty, Amier WildEagles99, Bunny Nakamoto-Kwan, Deirdre Hegarty, Lisa Keating, Owen Mark, JE Talent, Kathryn Abelson, Kim Steppe, David A. Heiman, Keith McLane, Karen Kemby, and JP Mark, my talented and ever-patient collaborator.

I thank my San Jose State University Theatre Arts Department graduate school committee advisor Dr. Kathy Kratochvil, who encouraged me to substantiate my theory and codify the methodology. I thank Dr. Alison McKee, Dr. David Price Terry, Dr. David Kahn, Kimberly Peterson Braun, and Elissa Mondschein.

My family and friends were patient and supportive throughout the development of this project, especially my daughters Brenden and Kendall, to whom I am extremely grateful. I am indebted to my late parents, my mother, who made me her buddy in the love of the Arts, and my father who said, just at the perfect moment, "You're an entrepreneur. You'll think of something."

Last, but not least: I thank Bill Starbuck. You are the wind beneath my wings.

Foreword
by Alan Arkin

Billie is the real deal. I met her first when she attended one of my workshops. It was clear within half an hour that she had most of the tools necessary to do really good work. She threw herself into the exercises completely and was immediately engaging, attempting new things, connecting deeply with the other people and had no trouble trying on criticism... in other words, she was completely present and available. An asset for any environment. During the course of the workshop, she so committed herself to the exercises that I found myself inspired to change some of my approach. It wasn't willfulness on her part, but her ability to so fully commit to what was happening that, as a result, it allowed me to see what I needed to do to catch up. What transpired as a result of working with her completely changed the way I handle the second part of the workshops. Her book is like she is. No nonsense. Practical and honest. Emotionally available. She comes to the point easily and quickly with a lot of authority, and simultaneously can change her approach on a dime if the event or the person calls for it. Billie embodies what she teaches, which is saying a great deal.

Introduction

This book may not be for you. You may enjoy the heck out of presenting and succeed every time you get in front of an audience. You may not get the jitters, dry mouth, or panic attacks before you step out on a stage. You may never have disagreements within your workgroups, or have to speak with employees who feel unappreciated, confused, or disengaged. You may never have misunderstandings with your manager, family members, or friends. Close this book and give it to someone who can use it. It's not for you.

This book is for you if you are a businessperson who is accomplished, hardworking, and really busy. You may not relish speaking to large groups, or small groups, or one on one when there is conflict. Your nerves may hold you back from successfully voicing your opinion and getting that promotion. Or you may just actively hate public speaking. But, darn it, you are required to deliver quarterly board presentations or present your concept to yet another investor.

This book is for you if you want to learn how to alleviate fear, uncertainty, and doubt when speaking in public or private. It's about confidently saying what you need to say to influence others. This book will help you improve your communication skills and successfully reach more of your goals.

If you are bringing me in to help your employees or team members deliver more effective presentations or collaborate better, this book will help them understand my methods in more detail.

For those people whom I have already trained, this book can serve as a useful reminder of the lessons and techniques we covered. Perhaps it will be a reference for how to calm nerves, collaborate with others, or clarify intention (i.e., objective). For others, it will offer a more in-depth understanding of the process.

For those who simply picked up this book to get some pointers, I hope you will find a thought or a technique that ignites a spark in you which alleviates any fear or self-doubt you have about speaking in public. I know you're afraid. I hope this book helps you to say it anyway!

Thirty years of acting in theatre, film, and commercials while teaching thousands of other actors gave me personal experience and insight into the fears and obstacles of performance anxiety. Around 1999, I was invited to conduct presentation skills workshops throughout the Silicon Valley business community. Very early on, I recognized the ever-present problems with participants' abilities to speak effectively and present ideas clearly. I saw that, unlike actors, corporate presenters had no process to overcome their inability to make worthwhile presentations. I had an aha moment. I could help these speakers! I could help them and the process wouldn't be complicated. I realized that, like actors, business speakers needed to manage their nerves, be more in touch with their feelings, cultivate body awareness, and develop audience connection. I was inspired to introduce more acting methods, adapt them for business, and blend them into my presentation skills teaching. I quickly discovered that the techniques used with actors worked equally well with business speakers!

My Process

Many major Silicon Valley companies hire me to help them in one of two ways, in either private sessions or group sessions. When I'm brought in to work privately, it's usually because individuals have very specific issues or circumstances that are getting in the way of them being their best presenters, leaders, executives, or communicators. At our first meeting, I do a diagnostic session with them, which usually lasts two hours, during which I explain the components of 'present-moment awareness'; this is followed by them telling me a story or giving me an abbreviated presentation. From that, I can tell what they're doing well and what is getting in the way of their being their best. After my diagnosis, the question I always get is, "How long will it take for you to fix the issues you identified?" The answer is that it usually takes three to six one-on-one meetings. After we work together, sometimes I shadow them and see how they're actually doing in meetings or during presentations. At other times we schedule a six-month or twelve-month tune up.

When I'm brought in to work with groups of ten to sixteen people at a company, I usually schedule two consecutive half-days (four-hour segments). My program is simplified, but the implications for each individual are extremely deep. To internalize and synthesize all that information, it helps if they have a night to digest and sleep on it. Sometimes individual private sessions are called for, especially if someone has a high-stakes presentation coming up.

The aim is to remove fear and replace it with techniques that give the speaker confidence in themselves. It is through that process their creativity is set free.

About the Book

This book describes my methods in detail and provides a useful framework for people who are planning to take my course. The chapters follow the same sequence of key concepts and interactive exercises applied in the workshops: Honesty, Body, Voice, Intention, and then the convergence of those ideas and individual insights through the practice of Improvisation. Each individual concept builds on the next and adds more context and rigor around the central theme that runs through all my training, namely *present-moment awareness*, which is the essential element to communicating effectively.

This book is organized around the three core facets of presentation influence: Your Self, Your Audience, and Your Message. In each case, if you want to fully understand what is to come in each section, I encourage you to read the Prefaces. In my experience, repeated exposure to concepts and ideas helps people remember and apply information better, so the Prefaces will give you the big picture.

If you just picked up the book to grab some pointers, or if you've already taken my program and need a refresher, I suggest you visit with the following chapters:

Chapter 2—Body: Learn a breathing technique to relieve your nerves.

Chapter 3—Voice: Vocal exercises to assure that you're heard and understood.

Chapter 11—Obstacles: Impromptu Q&A technique to help you confidently respond to those dreaded spur-of-the-moment questions.

Truth & Privacy

I'm devoted to working with businesspeople. My clients work hard and aren't expecting it all to happen for them without putting in considerable effort. I'm their coach, trainer, tutor, guide and, when necessary, drill sergeant. While our work together can be therapeutic, I am not a therapist. But, exactly like a therapist, I consider confidentiality and privacy to be paramount. Throughout this book, I relate stories of people I've worked with, but I purposefully don't mention actual names or companies. Occasionally, I created composites from participants with common experiences and circumstances. I've earned my clients' trust and I protect it.

I want my clients to succeed as much as they want to themselves. My value add is that I give them an unbiased and critical review to help them improve.

"You were great!" Everyone wants to hear that, but it's not always true. And when it's not, and people think it is, it creates a false sense of security. I won't give false praise, I won't accept excuses, and I won't tell someone they're great if they aren't.

Which doesn't mean I'm harsh or unfeeling. Quite the opposite. It is because I want my students to succeed that I am unwilling to be anything other than 100% honest with them. If I tell you "You were great," you can trust me—you were!

When we're working together, truth and honesty are what will take us to a higher plane of communication. I believe that all great work in any domain comes from a base of honesty, and it is for that reason that I begin each workshop, and this book, by building off that central idea.

Part I

Your Self

Preface to Part I

Every one of us has the potential to be great at presenting in front of an audience. It's a skill, a craft, an art, and fortunately, it's something you can learn.

Thirty years of performance and teaching experience have convinced me that when a performer or speaker delivers their message from within an awareness of the present moment, the whole of them will communicate efficiently and energetically. Successful communication occurs from the truth of that moment.

For years, I taught actors how to give better performances on theatre stages. Now I teach businesspeople how to give better presentations on company stages. The same skills, techniques, and approaches work equally well in both arenas.

Over the next five chapters in Part I, I will help you focus on your Self and the qualities you need to think about to be your best self on stage. These are basic performance mechanics that are easy to understand but require dedicated practice to be useful to you.

Learning the mechanics of acting through my exercises will help you develop an understanding and keen awareness of your senses and a more refined physical awareness of self, inside and out of your body. This self-awareness will improve breath control, eye contact, and audience connection. The mastering of these basic skills will demonstrate when you're living and participating in the present moment.

You will be able to free yourself from the burdens of fear and self-doubt while presenting. You will advance to a more sophisticated level of communication and expression, freeing up your creative imagination, using your personal style. Your message will be more fully experienced and shared with the audience.

After talking about honesty, a precondition for every great performance, I will describe the four components of present-moment awareness in great detail. In brief and in summary below, they are Body, Voice, Intention, and Improvisation.

Body: It is crucial to understand and experience how your body and your awareness of the present moment play vital roles in presentations and communications. My workshops begin with a simple and effective breathing exercise that delivers participants into the present moment. We practice that breathing exercise each time we meet.

Voice: You will learn the basic mechanics for using an effective voice, including exercises to teach effective diction, enunciation, projection, and voice modulation.

Intention: Having a specific intention aids in the manageability of fear, nerves, and self-consciousness while in front of an audience. We also focus on the basic mechanics of choosing an intention (an objective) and connecting it to a strong feeling. . . something you care about.

Improvisation: The improvisation exercises allow you to learn by doing. This process provides a safe place to play, fail, improve spontaneity, and establish successful connections with others.

The art of presentation influence begins with understanding each of the four components of present-moment awareness and then practicing them. The more you practice, the more confident you'll be. There is no limit to how influential a presenter you can become; the only limitation you face is yourself.

Need to get out of your own way? Let's go!

Chapter 1

Honesty

"The most courageous act is still
to think for yourself. Aloud."

—Coco Chanel

When I work with people, I do so using an artistic process, and it starts from the inside out. For the process to succeed, we need to agree when something works and when it doesn't. I am direct, and I tell people when it's working and when it isn't. I am always honest with them.

When it's not working, that means I don't believe or trust their presentation or I'm not experiencing a connection. The message doesn't match with what they're presenting externally or internally. Dishonesty in performance creates a disconnect. Decades worth of experience allows me to spot dishonesty in their performance instantly.

It's important to understand that honesty and truthfulness are not the same things. Being honest means not telling lies while being truthful means actively making known the full truth of a matter. If a speaker unknowingly says something that isn't true, they can still be speaking honestly.

Let us leave it to philosophers, lawyers, and religious leaders to determine what truth is or is not. That is not this book. I am an actor and have spent my career believing that honesty

13

is vital to all performances, presentations, and communications. I believe that an honest connection to what you're saying creates a chemistry uniting you and the audience on an emotional and intuitive level. When you are speaking honestly, you become relatable. Your performance will make the audience think, question, and reflect. You will encourage and comfort them, facilitating successful communication. Honesty is the ultimate service to your audience.

At the start, you may not recognize how it feels when your communication style is dishonest and coming across as insincere. You're using your old habits, and they still feel right. I will call you out on any artificial behavior. I will ask you to describe how you're feeling in that moment. From there, I'll implement an adjustment to address your feelings on the spot and begin to move you toward a more honest place. I will train you to recognize honesty within yourself, find a way to connect with your story or information, let the audience in, and, most importantly, not let fear get in your way. That's how we begin to move this artistic process forward.

It will be you and me working together to align in the present moment, which requires your assessment of how you're feeling before and after the adjustments. You will learn to feel and report concisely and clearly.

Yes, that is a tall order.

A creative collaboration requires that you permit yourself to be open to my feedback. You might feel vulnerable. It may feel a bit scary. Our relationship is built on collaborating in this safe place, building trust. When you are not authentic during your presentation, I will guide you. My methods are successful when we establish complete honesty with one another.

To improve your presentation skills, whether you're working with me or on your own, you must learn to start from a place of honesty. Your improvement will be stifled until you're able to objectively know what is working within your communication style and what isn't.

Honesty Is Beautiful

I often use the word "beautiful" to tell a client or student they presented well. Again, without getting too philosophical, I believe beauty comes from a place of honesty. I see the inherent beauty in people. It's a gift. I can see it radiating from inside people. I'm also able to recognize and identify what's getting in the way and inhibiting clear communication. Often it is an inauthentic connection with others—possibly masking nerves or a fear that's underneath.

When you walk on stage or in front of a room and you're fearful, your body language and behaviors will give you away every time. Emotional distress will manifest itself in the way you randomly pace, rock back and forth, tap your feet, talk too fast, talk too much, or hold a fake smile. Those are some of the manifestations of dishonest communication, and they stem from fear and nerves.

My process involves chipping away at those fearful cover-ups—using acting techniques to let the authentic you shine through your personal style.

The chipping away can be a dicey proposition at first. My clients are educated, accomplished, ambitious individuals who are driven to advance. If someone around them was brave enough, they were told that something about their presentations, communication, or influencing skills is hindering them. They have an idea that their presenting skills need improvement, but they are not clear on how to adjust. At first, they may not take kindly to me when I call attention to their inauthentic moments. But when their words and actions don't match, I am obliged to be honest and state my perspective. By doing so, I exhibit honesty by example and become a trusted source.

Kevin Systrom, a cofounder of Instagram, was recently on the Tim Ferriss podcast and spoke about his struggle with getting people to give him honest feedback about his presentation skills.

> I definitely started in a place where I just didn't listen to feedback. I was headstrong. Then as you have more and more failures—that, by the way, everyone has—you begin to realize it's really important to collect that data and that information from people. No one would tell me when I was presenting on stage. Everyone would be like, 'Great talk! Great! Awesome job! Great! You killed it!' It's like, that's not possible.
>
> A few talks in a row that happened. Then we hired someone. . . who came up to me after and gave me. . . feedback. I was like, 'Oh, my God. That person is right.' They literally watched every single interview I had done for the last two years, and just had a list of things. I was so grateful for that because it was feedback that no one else would give me.

Often, when people bring me in for training, they realize there is a problem and, like Kevin Systrom, they are open to feedback and change, but not always. In the twenty years that I've been conducting corporate presentation training, I've had two instances where the participants could not or would not rise to the required level of honest self-examination.

Some years ago, I worked with a law firm in Sacramento where the training was a well-regarded success. That firm recommended me to the head of Learning and Development for a Chicago law firm that then hired me to work with a group of six intellectual property lawyers.

The group I worked with in Chicago could not, or would not, take constructive feedback. Their reticence surprised me. The Sacramento firm's lawyers committed fully to each exercise. They accepted my comments and made great strides improving their presentation skills, but the participants in Chicago never did. The only difference I could see was that the group in Chicago exhibited high-powered, polished egos, while the lawyers in Sacramento were openly receptive and eager to improve.

Throughout the workshop, I saw a modest improvement in the Chicago group, but they continually resisted the exercises or my suggestions that encouraged them to be less cognitive and more in touch with their feelings. Perhaps the intimacy of being vulnerable among their colleagues was too threatening, or they viewed the process as too "touchy-feely." Either way, I was disappointed for them. They could have had much better results.

In the second case, I was employed by a VP of HR to help a senior manager of an online services company. I was told she had a few minor flaws that needed addressing. On the surface, it seemed straightforward. The VP of HR said the executive spoke too fast and in a monotone while presenting. I had many exercises and techniques for dealing with both issues, so I accepted the job.

Unfortunately, nothing I offered worked. I tried several techniques and gave the client various options to take corrective actions, but she staunchly refused to implement any of them. Worse still, for both of us, she became argumentative! When I tried to correct her monotone (because it bored her listeners), she said, "No one has ever told me I was monotone before." When I suggested exercises to address how fast she was speaking, she said, "Well, my friends understand me."

What is the value in arguing with a presentation coach whose sole purpose is to help you succeed? Halfway through our session, I had to pull the plug. I told her this particular process didn't seem to be working for her. I couldn't help her if she wasn't willing. I let her go with good wishes and reimbursed the company retainer. If it's not working, I want to be using my energy where it IS working.

I mention these two instances because they stand out, not as failures, but as examples of what happens if you attend my training sessions with a closed mind or heart. If you think your presentation skills are just fine, then this book or other coaching efforts will not be effective. If you think you're already polished, you'll be starting from a place where the chances of improvement are greatly diminished if not impossible.

To make progress, you'll need to approach this process with a willingness towards self-reflection and an openness towards authenticity that requires rigorous self-honesty.

The Arc

Storytelling is central to our lives and culture; indeed, the most successful among us are often those who excel at telling stories. At the beginning of each new speaker training session, I conduct the following exercise: The Arc. The exercise intends to get you up in front of the audience telling a familiar experience within a story-telling context. There are no words or facts to forget or mess up. It's your story!

In every book, movie, and stage play that is character-driven, there needs to be the framework of an arc present. The main character starts at the beginning, something happens in the middle, and by the end, they are someplace new, which could be either a physical place or an emotional one—new knowledge gained.

The instructions to the exercise are simple: You are asked to think about your story as though you're setting up a simple dramatic play.

Act One: You set the scene and introduce your audience to the setting, characters, and circumstances leading up to the event.

Act Two: You introduce the event or conflict that occurred.

Act Three: You resolve a problem, relating what was learned or how you changed.

The story needs a beginning, middle, and end and only needs to be two to three minutes in length.

The last instruction is the inclusion of your intention. I tell you that the reason you are telling me this story is to TEACH me something. I've made it simple for you: Your intention is the need to teach me something that you learned from your experience.

To give students a nudge, I share a brief personal story, such as when I taught my daughters to ride a bike, or the time I was in a car accident. My example is a minute or two long. I use it to demonstrate that things happen in life, and we are changed and learn new things as a result of those experiences. My intention is to teach you something from my story.

Once you think of a story, understand your intention, and have your beginning, middle, and end, you will have context, which means you'll have a story structure that will make it easier for your audience to follow you. The exercise is not established to judge you or your story. As your coach, I am there to support you in the way that *you* tell the story.

What is important is that your storyline must have a structure, but beyond that, you are free and encouraged to tell your story as you see fit. It could be about anything—a wedding, the birth of a child, a divorce—but it should be personal; it needs to have some personal meaning to you. That personal meaning is the catalyst to free your imagination and connect your entire being to the storytelling experience.

In the past two decades, I have heard hundreds of personal stories. The truth is I forget most of the stories moments after hearing them. I don't focus on the content; I'm interested in the feeling and emotional aspect of the storytelling. My work, my goal, is to facilitate students to be in the present moment and experience what that feels like. The process of telling a personal experience with a clear story that includes an arc helps anchor the mind to the body.

There is, however, one story that has stayed with me many years later. Ned, the vice president of a tech company in Seattle, Washington, hired me because he had trouble motivating his team. He wanted to get better at making presentations to become a better leader and inspire his group. His story was one he had never told anyone, and which came back to him as he began telling it. It was about a time when as a kid he went hiking with his dad.

Ned's dad was a single-minded person, critical and demanding. He had a man's stride and was a fast hiker. Little Ned could not keep up. He kept falling further and further behind. Like other times with his father, he couldn't open his mouth to tell his dad what he needed. He was unable to tell his dad to slow down.

At last, Ned was so far behind that, out of desperation, he knew he had to do something or risk getting separated. His dad was so intent on maintaining his fast pace that he didn't notice his son struggling. In a booming voice, Ned yelled to his dad, "STOP!" His dad stopped, turned around, and waited.

Ned told the story with great intention and with such a loud voice that his words brought tears to his eyes. He had been so angry all those years ago that his dad failed to notice him falling further and further behind. He felt sad that little Ned had so much difficulty speaking up.

His own words, right after he said them, had a therapeutic effect. At that moment, he realized that to accomplish certain things, he had to speak up! He also realized he had to speak effectively, sincerely, and in an appropriate manner. If little Ned had stated his need earlier, he might not have needed to shout. That was the lesson he learned from that experience.

Now years later, and in the safety of our training session, Ned at that moment realized that he didn't need to be afraid to express his needs. He didn't need to be frightened, weak, or timid when presenting to his company's employees because his intention was set: his words could help his team collaborate better.

The story of Ned's childhood hike with his dad dredged up old memories and awakened feelings of self-realization and empowerment. His self-honesty made him open to feedback and led to massive improvement. After our work together, Ned became a courageous, entertaining presenter. He learned how to harness that self-knowledge, and he now conveys meaningful messages to his audiences and coworkers.

When we start from a place of honesty, improvement always happens. To get better at public speaking, or any skill for that matter, you must be prepared to accept feedback. In the next chapter, we'll see how your honesty directly affects your body, and how that self-knowledge can immediately make you a better speaker.

Chapter 2

Body

"Remember to breathe.
It is, after all, the secret of life."

Gregory Maguire

Take a Deep Breath

I start every class I teach and every private coaching session with a simple breathing exercise. The work starts with the body, from the inside out.

The way I learned acting was from the inside out, which means getting present inside myself, within the present moment. That's how I teach it.

Your breathing is *critically* important.

It takes no more than 4 minutes. Here is how it goes:

Find a private place. Sit. Close your eyes.
Visit the SPEAKERS page on **www.billieshepard.com** for an
audio recording of this guided meditation.

- Take a big, deep breath in. Release through your mouth. *Notice any tension in your body. Give your body permission to relax.*

- Take a big, deep breath in. Release through your mouth. *Focus on your ears. What are you hearing in the present moment?*
- Take a big, deep breath in. Release through your mouth. *Remember something you heard this morning, then return to the present.*
- Take a big, deep breath in. Release through your mouth. *Focus on your eyes. Remember something you saw this morning.*
- Take a big, deep breath in. Release through your mouth. *Go inside to wherever you feel your emotions reside. What emotions are you feeling in this present moment?*
- Take a big, deep breath in. Release through your mouth.
- Tighten your toes and feet. Release.
- Tighten your toes, feet, thighs, and rear. Release.
- Tighten your toes, feet, thighs, rear, and stomach. Release.
- Tighten your toes, feet, thighs, rear, stomach, chest, hands, shoulders, face—every muscle. Release.
- Take a big, deep breath in. Release through your mouth.
- Take a big, deep breath in. Release through your mouth.
- Bring your awareness back into the room, opening your eyes.

After I complete this exercise in a group, this is what happens: everyone slowly opens their eyes and they all look like they just woke up from a thirty-minute power nap. Then I ask, "Is anybody aware of different feelings?" and they'll say things like, "I see more clearly," or "I'm more relaxed."

Then I'll ask, "Where in your body do you feel more relaxed?" They'll say, "In my shoulders," or "In my chest." So, they're getting in touch with their body from the inside.

In my Master's Thesis, *The Actor Within: An Exploration of Present-Moment Awareness in Business Presentations*, I wrote about one of my students whom I called "Jane," one of the most introverted and terrified people I have ever encountered.

> "Jane came to the class with an extreme fear of public speaking and little presentation experience. At the first class meeting, she sat unsmiling with eyes averted. During introductions she exhibited a tense body posture. Her shoulders were hunched forward and her arms were crossed. She had a withdrawn personality, showing little or no emotion. She expressed almost no reaction to the comments of other class members. When asked a question directly, her face would flush and she would answer as briefly as possible with a weak, monotone voice. Field notes indicated that Jane, who was the most shy and introverted at the first class meeting, showed improvement in vocal projection, spontaneity and clarity."

By the end of her training, Jane was the most improved speaker and became almost a different person. It turned out that what helped her most was the breathing exercise. She used the breathing exercise to put herself in the present moment and the results were spectacular.

The breathing exercise is the most effective way I know of to get people into the present moment and in touch with their bodies. It's amazing how shallowly most of us breathe and what a big difference such a small change can make.

For some reason, some people are embarrassed or self-conscious about breathing. It's incredible how withdrawn, restrained, and frightened people are to even take a deep breath. Extraordinary! But once they start taking deep breaths, they immediately notice a difference. If you want to give outstanding presentations on stage, *always* start with this breathing exercise.

Nervous Energy

Stan was typical of the CEOs I have worked with in the past. He was an alpha male, Type A, no-holds-barred leader who commanded respect by dint of his personality and 6'4" height. If you met him, you would be impressed. He had excellent people skills that he practiced with great finesse. He articulated his needs clearly and could make people feel heard. But in front of an audience, when he was presenting, his finesse vanished.

The problem Stan had, that many people struggle with, was an abundance of nervous energy. He couldn't stand still. On stage, he paced like a lion. His back and forth movements were at first mesmerizing but quickly became distracting. He gave the impression words could come out of his mouth only if he stayed in motion. He might not admit he was nervous on stage, but his body told a different story.

Nervous body energy manifests in all kinds of ways:

- Pacing
- Constant hand movements or repetitive gestures
- Stepping backward and then stepping forward
- Repeatedly touching the face or neck
- Arching the head to expose the neck
- Locked knees
- Unconsciously playing with hair
- Curling hair behind an ear
- Excessive smiling

If you've watched someone on stage you would label "nervous" then you've observed one or more of these "tells," or something similar. Like a poker player whose body unconsciously signals the cards they have in hand, public speakers can suffer from the same malady. They can't seem to help themselves. They generally aren't aware that they're demonstrating these "tell" behaviors.

Who's going to inform the charismatic CEO that his onstage pacing is driving people to distraction? Luckily for him, the company's VP of Communication was astute enough to know a change was warranted and called me in for a consultation.

When clients go off track during a presentation, exhibiting these nervous affectations, it is my practice to stop them right in their tracks. I've learned that adjusting at the moment works best with these distracting habits. In Stan's case, that was about twenty-two seconds into his first presentation.

"Stop!" I commanded.

He turned to look at me, stunned.

"What do you mean?"

"Why are you pacing?"

"It helps me think," he offered.

"Can you think in one spot?"

"Probably."

"Well then, do that."

And so he tried. Because I needed to course-correct him every few phrases, his ten-minute presentation took almost half an hour to go through.

Stan's face was flushed, and his upper lip became a little sweaty. He even got intermittently pissed off. But, to his credit, he stuck with the process. I don't often stop and start people when they're acting or giving a presentation because the artistic process is a flow. It's like getting a text message alert in the middle of an important meeting; it completely breaks your concentration. In Stan's case, because I needed to adjust a habit, it was necessary. There is a huge difference between badgering a person during a creative process, which I would never do, and correcting an ineffective habit.

When I correct students and clients, I do it from a place of care and respect. I'm not trying to irritate, anger, annoy, or exasperate anyone, although those are emotions that can be triggered. To get clients to an authentic place and into a deep connection with their audience, I have to work through the nervous veneer they have constructed.

For my students to learn to start from a successful place when presenting, I need to keep the pacing lion in one spot, I need to keep the gesticulator's hands still, or I may need to take the nervous smile off someone's face every time I see it.

As a result, in this safe, professionally guided environment, the person on stage being critiqued can feel vulnerable. They discover they no longer need their nervous behaviors. The option of resorting to their previous habit is removed. The habit is no longer useful. When this happens, honest emotions come out. And if they feel frustrated or angry, so be it. It's normal to experience such emotions, and I don't discourage it. Quite the contrary, real frustration in the moment can be a sign that someone is present and focused. The artificial nervous affectations dissipate. They are replaced by honest feelings and confidence.

People who work with me are sometimes surprised that I am a force of nature when it comes to coaching. I don't have an intimidating physical presence, but my job is to challenge even the most powerful and successful business people when required.

For Stan to improve on stage, he needed me to challenge him. He hadn't been genuine presenting on stage until I brought him to that point. Once we were there, he needed reassurance that he was in a safe place. After diligent practice, when he felt safe, confident, and secure in himself, a very attractive part of his personality surfaced. Stan had a quick and appropriate sense of humor. He now felt comfortable enough to incorporate that part of himself into his presentations.

Expressing Emotion

A way people sometimes express emotion during the process of changing a nervous habit is through tears. When I work with different groups within a company, occasionally a new student will come to my sessions having spoken with a colleague who previously attended my workshops.

"Are you going to make someone cry?!?"

It's a fair question, but I reassure them it's not something I set out to do.

We can express emotions like fear, anger, and sadness when our bodies and minds are connected and we are present in the moment. To get someone to understand what it takes to deliver a compelling presentation, it is necessary for them first to understand and FEEL what it means to connect to their true inner self.

My structured classes are not therapy sessions, although there are similarities. To be able to present your true self to an audience, you have to be carefully guided to dig deep to understand what constitutes your core being. And, it is your unique core being that makes you brilliant. That is what we want to see from your presentation. YOUR style, YOUR take on the information.

Actors continually go through this process, and the more accomplished actors understand it is an integral part of the art form. You can't portray a powerful leader on stage unless you dig deep into yourself to create an honest, emotional connection with what your character is experiencing.

Can You Do This on Your Own?

We all have images of ourselves which may not be fully accurate. We may think we come across one way and can be surprised to find our self-perception does not match another person's opinion of us. Self-delusion comes with a price. If we have no idea whether our audience dislikes our performance, how can we ask for honest feedback? We are prone to make the same mistakes over and over. How can we learn from them and get better?

For example, when I encounter people who excessively smile when presenting, they are unaware of that behavior. A force within me says to them, "I'm taking away your smile."

It may sound trivial, but I assure you it is not. The nervous smile is a crutch. The speaker believes their friendly smile helps them get through their public speaking commitment. They want to be accepted and appreciated, so they smile. But an audience perceives fake smiles as signs of weakness. They don't trust them. Ultimately, someone who smiles excessively will not win over an audience because they make themselves an object of pity, not strength or resolution. Each phony smile they deliver depreciates the message.

When I take away someone's smile, it leaves them, not surprisingly, feeling vulnerable. This new experience might trigger a "fight or flight" response. Yes, they might tear up, giggle, cry, or get angry.

I've been doing this training for decades, so I know how to carefully guide a person from this tentative place to a place of confidence for change-worthy learning. I am extremely careful to make the experience rewarding and positive. Someone without my depth of knowledge and specific background shouldn't attempt to "'take away someone's smile" because it could activate unintended consequences. For this reason, I don't recommend doing this exercise unless you are working with a highly trained, experienced coach.

What about using video feedback to spot nervous habits? Yes, I sometimes use video with my students as it allows me to play sequences back and illustrate what they are doing well and what behaviors require correction or adjustment. This allows us to be on the same page. The student sees their work while seeing it through my eyes. It is best to have an experienced coach/mentor watching you perform, providing a balanced critique with a wise, impartial view of your performance. They must hold a safe space for encouraging growth and articulating improvement.

I've had students review their videotapes and be surprisingly oblivious to some things they are doing incorrectly. We see what we want to see, right? That's because our brains can make assumptions, especially with habits. It's better to work with a professional coach who can point things out.

No one becomes a great speaker in two easy sessions of three hours. It doesn't work that way. Like any other skill, public speaking gets better with directed and deliberate practice. Continuing to work as a professional actor and teacher, I worked with some fine acting coaches over the years. In fact, I had a particularly helpful coach in an acting workshop three hours a week, every week, for four years. Along the way, I grew in my craft and continued to get better. When I had a challenging audition, he was my first call. Just so you know, Leonardo DiCaprio, Charlize Theron, Brad Pitt, and countless other accomplished actors continue to work with their coaches.

Even if you're at the top of your field, it doesn't mean you can't find ways to improve. Reading this book, or working with me for a few hours, will absolutely help you to make a giant leap forward. But if you want to take your game to the next level, you should think about communications and speaking skills as a long-term investment in one's self, not a "set it and forget it" kind of thing.

Fixing Nervous Body Habits

After you're aware of nervous habits, will you be able to self-correct? How long will it take for you to break a nervous habit?

The truth is that it depends. In my practice, I find two or three sessions is usually enough to correct the most glaring and undesirable nervous body habits. Some people respond quickly while others may take a little time. Fixing a distracting habit, however, is one of the easiest ways to see a massive and immediate improvement in presentation skills.

There are excellent books on the subject of creating good habits and breaking undesirable ones, including *The Power of Habit* and *Atomic Habits*. In short, here is what you need to know about correcting nervous traits:

1. You must be aware of the habit in the first place. If you don't know you have a nervous smile, or you cock your head and show your neck to the audience in a vulnerable way, or you constantly use your hands, you won't be able to address and correct the problem.

2. Each time you experience the habit, which is known as the "cue," you must note it and correct it immediately. A cue leads to, or corresponds with, a specific behavior, often a craving, a response, and a reward, which is how a habit loop develops. You did something, whatever it was, and it led to a positive outcome (you succeeded). Therefore, you keep repeating it. Finding the specific cue that precedes the behavior allows you to retrain your brain. You develop new effective behaviors to associate with that cue.

3. You need to learn how to be present in the moment when you are called to make a live presentation. That's something I will teach you in Chapter 5 of this book. When you have mastered that skill, you will find that your nervous habits are no longer a concern. You will discover that being the most vibrant version of yourself is incredibly rewarding and vastly satisfying. This is a valuable, self-perpetuating positive feedback loop. Your nerves won't control you because you'll understand that fear and nerves take you out of being centered and present.

4. The nervous habits people pick up to help survive the stress of facing an audience are manifestations in the body. When you enter a place of being present, you'll experience the most amazing feeling of all: your body will be liberated, your gestures will be natural, and you will move without pretense, anxiety, or affectation. You will be free.

"Now. Breathe. In. . . and out.
In. . . and out. In. . . and out."

- From ***Laughing Wild***
by Christopher Durang

Chapter 3

Voice

*As an artist, the most important job I have
is to tell the story.*

Judy Kaye

Tony award winner Judy Kaye is a great actress. And she happens to have a remarkable voice!

We were drama-nerd classmates in high school and even then, it was undeniable that her voice was special. If you have a chance, download her version of "Ave Maria" or anything else she sings. Her voice and acting will move and inspire you.

It's impossible for me to say how much genetics and talent may or may not have played a part in Judy's sensational voice, but I do know that continued work and commitment played a part in taking whatever God-given ability she had to the next level, and to the level beyond that one.

When I asked Judy if she'd be willing to impart a helpful quote for this chapter on voice, she graciously nailed it: *"The number of octaves I can sing, combined with other skills, i.e. breath control and diction, help to tell the story and deliver the relevant emotions in the text."*

Likewise, as a business speaker your most important job is to tell the story! Your voice must be at your disposal to tell your story well.

We all have some natural vocal ability as well as the option to improve the quality of our voices. The only questions then are how important an influential speaking voice is to your career, and how hard you are willing to work to improve it?

When we hear someone speaking in a monotone voice, it's like listening to the same note over and over and over. . . . We lose interest quickly. Monotone speakers are capable of wider ranges, but they haven't been taught how to use their voices as an instrument. With proper coaching, they could use their voices to seduce and intrigue audiences rather than put them to sleep!

People may be born with vocal talent, but most of the great ones leveraged their gifts and learned how to craft a better version of themselves. Like Judy, they worked hard at it.

Think of Benedict Cumberbatch and his deep, resonant voice. Can you hear how melodious he sounds in your mind?

Now think of Anthony Hopkins. There's a musicality to his voice, isn't there? It doesn't hurt that his lilting British accent makes every word sound important.

My specialty includes teaching clients the most basic mechanics of voice and diction, and then guiding them through exercises designed to expand their vocal range and help them speak in a more purposeful manner.

The Mouse that Roared—Part I

When a soft-spoken student gets up in front of the class to speak and we can't hear them, if I say, "Speak up, we can't hear you!" what do you suppose happens?

They freeze.

For many speakers, the thought of speaking louder in front of an audience cripples their ability to focus on their message.

To teach a metaphorical timid mouse to roar in front of a group, two independent skills need to be addressed simultaneously.

First, I focus on the act of articulate speaking, using correct pronunciation and clear diction. Then I teach a specific process for speaking with intentional volume and confidence. The speaker learns how to differentiate between these two skills, practice them independently, and then integrate them.

I teach people how to speak more articulately using acting techniques and a variation on a method made popular nearly 2400 years ago by a Greek statesman named Demosthenes. According to legend, Demosthenes corrected his own speech impediment and learned to become a great orator by putting pebbles in his mouth and shouting above the roar of ocean waves. He also recited poetic verses while running with pebbles in his mouth.

I don't recommend running with pebbles in your mouth.

There is a simpler and less perilous method. My students are instructed to place a pencil lengthwise across their back molars and hold it firmly between their teeth.

In this exercise, with the pencil in place, students are asked to read aloud the poem *Music and Moonlight* written by English poet Arthur O'Shaughnessy.

> We are the music makers,
> And we are the dreamers of dreams,
> Wandering by lone sea-breakers
> And sitting by desolate streams;
> World-losers and world-forsakers

On whom the pale moon gleams:
Yet we are the movers and shakers
Of the world forever, it seems.

The magic within this O'Shaughnessy poem incorporates a musicality and rhythm that helps students find their natural voice.

To do this, try firmly biting down on a pencil across your back molars, read this poem aloud, pronouncing each word as clearly as possible. This will be training (working out) for your lips, teeth, and tip of your tongue. Pronounce each word with exaggerated enunciation and overly precise diction.

Warning: There isn't a way to do this exercise without a certain amount of slobber. So keep tissues on hand!

Practice one to two minutes at a time. Less than that won't be effective. More than two minutes can be too tiring for one session. If you want to practice more, do the exercise three to four times a day.

Take notice when any words or phrases inspire an image or feeling in you. Now you're incorporating the whole of yourself into the process. Because there is more time, I have my private students read aloud the Gettysburg Address as well. The pencil exercise slows them down, forcing them to pay attention to every word and phrase. Rarely does anyone get through it without getting emotionally affected.

Once you've completed this part of the exercise several times, repeat the process again but without the pencil. I guarantee your words will fly out of your mouth fluently and with greater precision.

It's so easy to develop poor speech habits. We get lazy. We mumble and swallow words without awareness. Unfortunately, we can behave like timid mice, giving shy, weak responses when we wanted to influence our listeners.

Don't give up. Practice like a career actor would practice. Commit to doing the pencil exercise before your next presentation. You will develop more vocal clarity and improve your ability to focus on the important messages you wish to communicate.

The "pencil in the mouth" exercise works. I've used it with great success in all of my workshops and private sessions. My students experience remarkable improvement and retain their ability to hone this important communication skill.

The Mouse that Roared—Part II

The pencil between the teeth exercise helps alleviate many diction and fluency problems, but the second vocal issue we work on is not speaking loud enough. Students are often not aware of how much volume they need to produce, and sometimes they don't understand why it's important. Volume and modulation are critical.

"Hey, I can just use a microphone, right?"

Maybe.

A microphone can be a crutch. If you use one all the time, you won't be able to get around without it. Furthermore, expanding your vocal options improves both the audience reception of your message and your enjoyment while delivering it.

What you may not realize is that volume control and self-confidence go hand in hand.

When you get up in front of an audience and speak with appropriate volume and clear articulation, you project greater confidence. And guess what? You will be more confident!

I've coached accomplished business people who began training with me speaking at a volume that qualified as a whisper. They didn't realize that their soft voice led audiences to discount much of what they said.

To help people understand how to project their voices with more volume and confidence, I use an exercise called "Throw Me the Ball™."

The exercise takes two people to start, but once you learn my method, you can practice by yourself. Here's the second exercise:

Imagine we're standing in a large room and I'm directly in front of you. Let's pretend your voice is a baseball. I'll ask you to "Throw me the letter A" with your voice. I'll hold out my hand and explain, "I'm wearing a baseball mitt, waiting for your letter A to arrive."

In the beginning, I'll stand a couple of feet away from you. Then I'll move a few steps further back, still holding out my hand. I'll ask you to throw that letter A right into my glove. To raise the danger level, I might ask you to throw the letter B. I'll move around the room, moving from side to side and further back each time. I'll keep asking for the "ball" to be thrown hard, vocally, right into my glove.

What happens?

You will experience your voice projecting. You will learn that when you want to throw a "ball" to the back of the room, you need to have enough air in your lungs. And, to accomplish that you'll need to engage your lungs and diaphragm to get LOUD. You will feel it. As simple as that sounds, it works!

Next, imagine that I've moved to the far back of the room. I have you read the O'Shaughnessy poem from Part I using the same level of volume as the baseball letters you pitched my way.

Having a coach or friend work with you is preferable. You'll get immediate reinforcement when improving and useful feedback when you're not. While I'm coaching, when someone achieves their volume goal, I say, "That's it! Remember how that feels!" And students confirm, even months later, that they remember! They remember because their actions and feelings are now tied to a physical experience.

By the way, I coach so many ESL and ESOL clients, and it's important to mention that a secondary benefit of the Pencil In The Mouth and the Throw Me the Ball exercises is that they greatly improve ESL (or third or fourth language) participants' delivery. Oftentimes one or both of these exercises solves any issues of being heard or understood because they slow down delivery and clean up pronunciation issues so the audience can clearly understand them.

The Land of Nod

"How do I know if I'm projecting my voice at the required level?"

There are signs: Look for what I call the "Land of Nod."

When an audience is connected to you, when they really hear your words and receive your message, you may see them nodding their heads. Nodding is a great affirmation from the audience.

Another sign that your message is landing effectively relates to how the audience sits in their seats. When they're leaning forward towards the stage with eyes on you, you can be sure they're 100% invested in what you're sharing.

"What happens if I'm not getting any reaction from my audience?"

Ask them! "Hey, guys (or ladies and gentlemen, or everyone), are you tracking with me? Can you hear me OK in the back?"

Feedback from your audience is key to addressing communication breakdowns. Do they seem disengaged? Are they looking at electronic devices and not paying attention? Are they avoiding eye contact with you? If any of these answers are yes, it's time to adjust the way you are transmitting your message. The audience is 50% of the experience!

Connecting is a major part of the joy of communicating with your audience. Practice having fun with these exercises. Remember your voice is an instrument and you can play it at various tempos, volumes, and cadences.

What do you suppose would happen if you smiled and were happy, then started reading the exercise poem loud enough that the imaginary folks at the back of the room could easily hear you? What would happen if you enjoyed making yourself heard?

To get better at speaking with confidence and projecting your voice successfully, it helps to train with a coach to get specific feedback and practice more advanced techniques. If you don't have a coach, you might enlist the services of a trusted friend, someone who will give you an honest assessment of your voice and performance. Without constructive criticism and lots of practice, improvement will likely be difficult.

Yes, It Takes Practice

It *will* take effort and discipline to practice the Part I and Part II exercises **before** any presentation. Take the time. Invest in yourself.

I advise blocking in ten extra minutes before leaving for your presentation to ground yourself, breathe, and review the vocal techniques you've learned.

Practice reading the O'Shaughnessy poem (or another piece you like) with a pencil between your teeth. Then take the pencil out and practice saying the poem loudly, as if you were throwing a baseball with your voice to the back of a room.

These two simple exercises, performed together, produce tangible results! I've seen it happen a thousand times, and it still thrills me to watch a timid mouse begin to roar!

Chapter 4

Intention
Conquering Fear

*"You must do the thing
you think you cannot do."*

Eleanor Roosevelt

Your boss insists you take a communications class. Public speaking is your worst nightmare. The last thought before you die might just be how horrible it is to speak in front of a crowd.

A surprisingly large number of people feel that way. My student Brigitte was one of them.

When the time came in the workshop for each participant to share a two-minute personal experience, Brigitte declined.

How could she decline? It's communications training! But she did.

She was so fearful that when I encouraged her to say even a couple of words, she could not. Zero words came out of her.

I've trained actors and businesspeople for decades. I've seen challenging cases before; Brigitte was in dire need of my expertise.

I understood her pain. I too had been a shy person once.

This terror is not something anyone can power through on their own. Throwing a child in the water to deal with their fear of swimming is both cruel and counterproductive. You've now created someone who has reason to be afraid because their worst nightmare just came true.

Let's start there.

Fear is real, palpable, and can be debilitating. It doesn't matter how smart you are, how good-looking, how talented, or even how much people like you. Anyone can have a fear of public speaking. And I can say to you with absolute assurance that anyone can learn to speak with confidence in public if they have a desire to do so.

In my practice, I have a variety of exercises and methods that I use with students. What works for some may not work for others. It's an intuitive process. No teacher has one magic formula that will work 100% of the time, but I have developed a wide range of processes tailored to meet individual needs that consistently work.

Which one or ones (in combination) will work depends on the individual.

There is always a method to get a student through that knot-hole of fear.

What worked for my student Brigitte is an exercise called "Chase the Demon," which I've used with great success in my acting and corporate workshops. It is just one of the many exercises I teach, selected from my Louis Vuitton coaching tool-kit bag!

Before I go any further, let me advise you that certain exercises should be practiced in a safe and comfortable group setting with an experienced facilitator who can skillfully guide you through specific processes. It is not easy for students to learn how to identify precisely where their personal blockages reside inside their body.

Chase the Demon

Imagine you're an actor and you've just been asked to step up on an empty stage. You're prepared and ready to act, improvise, or take direction to perform something. Now imagine that I instruct you to stand facing the audience and do. . . nothing.

All eyes are on you. The audience is waiting for you to do something, grateful it's not them up there. But you can't. You've been given no action, no intention, no façade. The only instruction I offer is "Stay with the moment."

As you stand there doing nothing, your mind racing, you will experience the naked fear that every actor feels at some point before performing. You might feel the tension in your jaw, butterflies in your stomach, tightness in your throat, sweaty palms, tight shoulders, or shaking knees.

There are few things more terrifying than standing on a stage and feeling an overwhelming sense of panic. The "fight or flight" response is real, and that screaming voice in your head wants you to escape to safety NOW.

Not so fast.

Gut it out and stand there. Focus on your body. Once you've been directed how to identify the specific distressed body part, you'll be instructed to say out loud where you are feeling the tension. You'll be told to breathe deeply into that area of your body. It's a grounding process. You will chase that demon from each body part until, finally, it gives up and leaves your body. Where does it go? Most likely it's residing in the guy next to you, making him nervous! In that moment you will have chased away the nerves by rerouting your thinking patterns while in front of an audience.

This exercise demonstrates that with intention you can have control over your nerves. You learn through experience that you can stand in front of an audience and the world will not end. The fear may be there, but the fear can be tamed and even eliminated.

In my class, I asked Brigitte to stand up, walk to the front of the room, stand there, and do nothing.

"Do you feel nervous?" I asked.

All you had to do was take one look at her to know she was nervous.

"Yes," she said.

"Where do you feel nervous?"

I knew from the way she was standing, shoulders slouched and pinched inward, that she was trying to make herself smaller.

"Do you feel tight in your shoulders?"

"Yes," she said timidly.

"Take a deep breath in. Move that breath into your shoulders. Can you do that?"

She closed her eyes and took a deep breath. I saw her concentrating, and her shoulders gradually began to loosen. "Good. Now take another deep breath and keep your eyes open this time." She kept herself inside the process, following my directions. I could see the audience relax along with her.

"Do your shoulders feel better?" She said they did. "What about now? Where do you feel the nerves in your body? Do you feel nervous in your stomach?"

"Yes."

"Take another deep breath in. Breathe deeply into your stomach. The fear will run away from there, too."

Her hands were fidgety. I asked her to do the same exercise with her hands. Once we had chased the fear all around her body, she noticed something remarkable.

She was relaxed.

Her face was relaxed. Her body was relaxed. She was "present" and "in the moment" with her classmates without feeling fearful. The demon was gone from her body. We all saw the transformation and saw only a calm person standing before us.

It took five minutes—start to finish—five minutes. From there, Brigitte learned that she could stand in front of an audience and chase fear from her body. She was actually in control! Her *intention* was to identify the physical source of her anxiety, and when she accomplished that she also managed to tame her fear.

This is crucial: Becoming clear on your intention, whatever that intention may be, is the first and most important step in managing fear, becoming present on stage, leading a work-group meeting, preparing to ask your boss for a raise, or having a conversation with your teenager! But, that's another story. Embroider this on a pillow if it helps you remember: "What the heck is my INTENTION?"

Fear Is Manageable

Nearly everyone faces fear and anxiety when getting up on a stage, whether it's for a school play, facilitating a work group or delivering a high-stakes presentation. It's my experience that most actors started out feeling shy and fearful.

This is what Academy Award-nominated actor Emily Blunt said in a recent NPR interview about her first performance in front of an audience:

> I was scared. I'll never, ever forget the first time I went on stage in front of the public. It was my first job, and I was eighteen, and I was in a play in the West End, and I just was sweating bullets. I was so

frightened! I felt like I was ten paces behind myself trying to catch up all night. Out of body—literally out of body experience. I'll never forget that feeling.

So yes, it's completely normal to feel that way. And it hasn't stopped Emily Blunt from becoming one of the most sought-after actors of our time. She certainly learned how to manage her fear.

Here is what another two of the best, American stage director and founder of the American Conservatory Theatre (ACT) William Ball and Academy Award winner Alan Arkin, have to say about intention.

William Ball said while addressing the importance of intention in his book *A Sense of Direction*, "The only real reason a director is needed in rehearsal is to perform the following function: persistently to draw the actor to a more meaningful and appropriate choice of objectives (intentions), and then to persuade the actor to lend his full commitment to those objectives." Like all fine directors, Ball recognized that authentic performances on stage occur when an actor connects and commits to his intention. Committing to an intention seems to flip a switch somewhere deep within the brain, turning empty spoken words into full expression. When actors or corporate presenters connect with their intention, they no longer feel fear. Why? Because intention overrides fear.

Alan Arkin has a lot to say about intention. He acts with intention. He writes, directs, and teaches with intention. He lives his life with intention! Alan Arkin taught me more about intention in his improvisation workshops than any other teacher I ever experienced. He's a master. If he and his beatific wife Suzanne decide to offer their workshop anywhere near your continent, get there. If that's not possible, read *An Improvised Life*:

A Memoir or listen to *Out of My Mind*. You'll learn something that will improve your presentations, communications... and life. No exaggeration.

His workshops changed my life. With his enlightened instruction and kind, expert direction, through a series of personal improvisations, I was able to experience the power of intention more deeply than ever before. He describes my workshop experience in his book. I won't go into it here. Read his book, Chapter 17. You'll see I had a very clear intention, connected to a very strong feeling!

Back to the point. Alan says, "The first tool is *intention*, and once understood, the deal is that you never enter the playing area without your character having an intention, a specific job to do, a function to perform. This accomplishes several things. First, it makes it impossible to have stage fright or to be self-conscious. There isn't time. You have something to accomplish. Second, it allows you to be alive without self-judgment."

Wouldn't it be great to deliver your next business presentation without stage fright, self-consciousness, or self-judgment? To paraphrase Arkin: Never deliver your presentation without knowing your intention!

There are many ways to deal with fear on stage, but the most reliable way is to learn how to connect and commit to your intention. The Chase the Demon exercise demonstrates fear can be managed by applying the power of intention. Remember:

1. Your intention in this exercise is to identify your fear.
2. Recognize it in your body.
3. Acknowledge out loud where the fear is in your body.
4. Breathe into that fear and you will eliminate it.

Your body is your vessel, and you're in control.

That silly demon doesn't rule, you do.

Chapter 5

Improvisation

"One of the things I learned from impro-vising is that all of life is an improvisation, whether you like it or not. Some of the great-est scientific discoveries of the 20th century came out of people dropping things."

Alan Arkin

The thought of doing improvisation might intimidate some folks. It turns out the improvisation exercises are probably the most liberating, exciting, fun, rewarding, and confidence-building portion of my workshops.

At the very first session of every seminar, as we form a circle and before we do our breathing exercises, I explain the work-shop "setup."

"You are actors. You have been cast in this play. You're play-ing a role. I'm the director. This is our first readthrough and rehearsal. Work on our experiential play begins here."

It is important for students to identify as actors from the very beginning of the training. In this way, any adjustments I suggest are more accessible to them. They're more open to trying things a new way because we're all playing a role in a production. They don't take things personally because it's acting, and everyone knows that actors take direction and incorporate adjustments all the time.

People love to play, so my seminars are opportunities for them to play, explore, and learn. They learn the fundamentals of communicating in the present moment through play.

Students are provided a *place* to play, where they can feel safe and fail, and then realize that they're not going to die because they made a mistake or embarrassed themselves. Participants learn that every improvisation exercise has meaning. They experience all of the things that go into performing or speaking in a giving, authentic, and receptive way. Most importantly, they gain an awareness of the performance mechanics necessary for effectively communicating with other humans.

Think of it like lion cubs at play. When the cubs are playing, they're experiencing the mechanics of hunting or lying in wait, incorporating the information necessary for survival.

My students eventually understand it this way: If I can learn through play with these improvisation exercises, I'll be able to communicate better. If I'm averting my eyes while I'm communicating with somebody, I'm missing a huge amount of information I could be receiving back from the audience or the person I'm speaking with.

That lost information could make the difference between closing a sale or not! If I miss an expression that indicates my client doesn't understand what I'm saying, or that he needs more data than I'm delivering, I'm missing a lot of information. Through improvisation, we are taught to pay attention. Improvisation provides a safe place to fail, learn, relearn, and experience.

It Starts with Games

The basic improvisation exercises happen before my students are even thinking about writing their ultimate workshop presentation. This process gives them the chance to experience and embody the performance mechanics so that by the time they get to deliver their presentation, they have learned to manage their fear, increased their self-confidence, and gained the techniques to apply to their presentation delivery.

I've discovered that it doesn't take all that much time to embrace these basic mechanics. This methodology employs a practical method sufficient for immediate and lasting learning.

The next time they get up before an audience and realize they're not making eye contact, they'll actually realize they're not making eye contact and adjust the problem on their own. Or they'll realize they're not breathing deeply and they'll take a big deep breath. Through improvisation exercises, students have internalized the mechanics of effective communication and the ability to self-correct.

Note that improv is different from improvisation.

When somebody says they're doing improv, that's a different thing from improvisation. Improv is a form of live entertainment characterized by improvisation and interaction with an audience, often with a goal to be funny.

Improvisation is the ability to improvise in the present moment using what's at hand to move forward in communicating in an authentic way.

Improvisation exercises change lives because once you have experienced truthfulness in a present moment, everything else is a facsimile. Secondarily, once you experience observing another person being in the present moment, you have a greater awareness of when they're *not*. That discerning ability to recognize it in oneself and in another changes how people communicate. We can often sense who's being authentic and who's not. We might better know who to trust and who not to trust.

People tell me many times after our workshops that, "I no longer attend [a certain organization] because their stated goals weren't being supported. I couldn't trust them." Or "After I learned to be in the present moment, I finally ended a relationship with someone who continually lied to me."

For whatever reason, the byproduct of improvisation training is that it helps students get into the present moment. It also serves the purpose of creating a filter that allows them to recognize inauthenticity in others. I didn't set out to create that dual purpose. The fact is that these communication techniques have other applications.

The Mechanics of Improvisation

It sounds counterintuitive to say that improvisation requires specific mechanics. Isn't improvisation supposed to be spontaneous? Isn't it all extemporaneous? No, not exactly.

Every exercise I apply in the workshops is selected carefully to achieve the result that will most benefit the presenters. The variations are endless, but when I teach improvisation techniques, I lean heavily on three preeminent masters of the art: Viola Spolin, the improvisation coach who wrote the hugely influential book *Improvisation for the Theater*, known as the bible of improvisational theatre; Alan Arkin, who is at the pinnacle of acting and acting coaches and needs no further introduction; and Patsy Rodenburg, who created the concept of the Second Circle that I explain in detail in the next chapter.

Each teacher has a slightly different explanation for how improvisation is a key to present-moment awareness, and each uses a slightly different technique. Which is the best? They're all great!

What Spolin, Arkin, and Rodenburg did was to create a rich set of improvisation tools, each of which may be applied to different people or groups at different times, depending on their needs. The beauty of the exercises is that they have been refined, tested, improved, and confirmed to work over many decades. I've learned one exercise might work better than another for some workshop groups. Let me give you an example.

If I become aware that a workshop group is lacking consensus about a project, there are improvisation exercises to practice spontaneous planning! I might ask eight students to "Hang a big picture." I set the scene. "You work in a museum. You've been instructed to hang a painting. It is twelve feet wide by eight feet tall. It must sit on the wall perfectly straight and not be damaged in any way."

Let me tell you—this ain't easy!

What students learn in this group improvisation exercise is how to think creatively, communicate effectively, collaborate, and reach consensus. Predictably, when a group of students has a single task to accomplish, every individual has their own idea on how to do it.

Want to see an argument? Assign a single task to a married couple. Instantly each person will begin to apply their own idea. The "hang a picture" improvisation exercise elicits similar emotions in workshop groups.

The extrovert will often start talking first and everybody else will listen. But as he continues on, he'll notice other members of the group aren't listening to him. They're listening to someone else in the group who may be more introverted. To get cooperation and succeed at the task, they have to look people in the eyes and listen carefully. They discover that not cooperating turns out to be a waste of valuable time.

Almost without exception, at first the introvert stands back and lets others offer ideas. One of the shy ones in the group finally says, "Well, we could use this bigger hammer and it would work better." No one wants to fail to hang the picture in front of their peers.

The picture will always get hung, and participants in the exercise will always stand back with pride and pat their backs. As a team, they collaborated, some of their ideas were accepted, they worked through their differences, and they accomplished their task. Mission accomplished! Aren't *we* great and wasn't that fun!

The major take-away from this and other improvisation exercises is that people learn to experience being in the present moment. They are forced to have to listen to others and be quiet. They learn when to speak up and when to listen, or they'll be in the museum until 4:00 a.m. still trying to hang the painting! The exercise ends when they've worked together and accomplished their task. The person who realizes that a heavier hammer will be more efficient *learns* to speak up. In order to succeed, each participant must get into the present moment where they have to listen and speak efficiently within mutual cooperation.

When the exercise is over, I don't lecture. To reaffirm their learnings, I ask questions like "What did you notice about your eye contact?" or "What did you feel when you finally spoke up?" There is more of an impact when participants make discoveries on their own and observe how their teammates succeeded or failed.

Sometimes I'll incorporate one-on-one improvisation exercises if the group needs it. In the following case, the group needed it. I recently did a seminar with a mix of hardware and software engineers. One engineer was painfully shy, eyes averted. His hands were fidgety and he talked so fast it was difficult to follow what he was saying. The other, a woman who was an extremely stoic director, had her own set of nervous issues. She spoke with a clenched jaw and tight neck and shoulder muscles. I selected an improvisation exercise for the purpose of connecting an intention with a strong feeling, which is key to unlocking the artistic process of communicating discussed throughout this book.

I simply told them their location and character. "You're both on a spaceship." I assigned them roles. "You're the captain," I told the shy engineer. And "You're the first officer," I told the stoic director. That's all I said. I gave them a couple of minutes to set their scene—not write a novel, just enough time to set a scene.

Usually, students in these cases begin by doing improv—and they want to be funny. They're self-conscious and they're trying to be funny to deflect their nerves in front of the group. I watched and waited to spot their intention or objective. I let them play for a while. Then at some point, I gently stopped the scene. I took each one aside individually.

I said to the captain, "That's a real nice start," because it was, "and I can see you're working on an intention." Then I pointed from his head to his solar plexus, saying, "Connect your intention to a strong feeling about that intention, here. Your feeling doesn't have to make sense. It doesn't have to relate to anything logical, necessarily. Maybe ask yourself why you're having this particular intention as the captain of this ship."

He looked at me straight in the eyes and calmly said, "Okay."

"Take your time. This is your time. Don't enter the play area (stage) until you're clear on your intention and it's connected to a strong feeling."

Next, I walked the first officer over to the side and privately said to her, "Nice job," because it was. "I can tell you were working on your job position. Now," pointing from her head to her solar plexus, I said, "Clarify your intention and connect it to a strong, personal feeling." I followed up with the same instructions. "Do not enter the play area until you have identified an honest feeling inside yourself."

This practice, to connect intention to a strong feeling, consistently improves a scene. Why? Because each participant begins listening to the other person! Why are they listening? Because they *have* to listen to the other person to make sure they achieve an intention that means something to them! This authentic listening promotes a realistic situation complete with natural pauses and authentic responses.

They began their scene again, and this time it turned into one of the most dramatic workshop moments I've witnessed. Even before they spoke everyone saw how deeply they were in the scene. Out of the blue, the first officer said, "Captain! I note a space vessel coming from coordinates 3-5-1 approaching at attack angle thirty-four."

The captain responded, "What sector is that?"

The first officer didn't have time to answer that question. Remaining calm, not wanting to express her terror, she said, "Captain, the space vessel is now coming in towards us at Warp 2 speed!"

The shy, nervous young software engineer suddenly dropped his head into his hands. "I never anticipated this occurring." And we knew he meant it! He was devastated.

The rest of the group sat there, riveted. The captain seemed emotionally incapacitated. What would happen next?

The first officer urged, "Captain! Get a grip on yourself!"

The captain sat up, got himself in control, and the scene continued for a bit longer. It was thrilling to watch the two committed space-professionals, dealing with this life-threatening circumstance.

The moment was remarkable.

I didn't want to, but I had to step in and continue the classwork. I gently stopped the scene and asked the class, "What did you observe that was different from the first runthrough?"

Audience members chimed in, "They were listening to each other!" and "They were super spontaneous!" and "It was very moving!"

The differences between take one (improv) and take two (improvisation: practicing intention connected to a strong feeling) were worlds apart. The result, which later carried over to the team's business presentations, was the same kind of dynamic tension we've all felt many times in great movies, theatre, and performances.

Shakespeare Was Right: We All Are Actors on a Stage

Because of my acting background, I sometimes assign character roles to people in my seminars. Why? Because underneath we're all actors, and because if you want to be excellent at presenting, you need to practice being an actor. When you're up on stage, it's very much like you're playing a role.

There are certain people who come to my workshops that I get a "hit" from. Once I work with people, I often see their special essence. This allows me to "cast" them as I might if

I were a casting director for a play or movie. After working through some of his defenses and becoming more present in the moment in front of the audience, one of my students struck me as "an angel," for his wonderful presence, intelligence, and authentic leadership ability. I said, "You're an angel." The class voiced its agreement; they saw it too. His nickname at the workshop became "Angel." As a side note, "Angel" continued to improve his presentation skills. He became such a fine speaker that he was invited more and more to share his knowledge, delivering influential presentations worldwide.

The captain in the spaceship scene had shared early on in the workshop, "I'm always nervous and tend to speak too fast. People have been telling me for years that I'm high strung." But, through improvisation, his personality evolved! The previously nervous and high-strung communicator-character died that afternoon and was replaced by the wise man! He became the elegant "Dalai Lama" and everybody in the group agreed that's who he was—a calm, poised, and serene Dalai Lama—and that persona carried over into his presentation work moving forward. By experiencing his truth in the moment, he realized being calm while communicating was possible and more enjoyable.

And the woman in the scene, the stoic director who played the first officer? Well, she struck me as "The General." She wasn't a general when she came into the workshop, but she found the character of The General once we worked together. Commanding leadership ability and energy were trapped inside of her, yearning to get out.

My use of nicknames isn't intentional and they don't always surface, but when they do, they seem to stick. Best of all, when people remember a pivotal quality about themselves, it becomes internalized and helps them play their actor's role while presenting. If I suggest a shy, soft-spoken young woman put on the crown and coat of a queen and enter the play area as that queen, the transformation can be stunning. When I identify positive characteristics and qualities of people who haven't yet noticed those qualities in themselves, they gain confidence.

This is why I love my work!

I am dedicated to helping people discover their potential and personal style. This process transforms someone from being an average speaker into a powerful presenter with unlimited opportunities to captivate and influence others.

Part II

Your Audience

Preface to
Part II

You may think that presentations are all about you because you're the one standing there facing an audience. In truth, the audience is a crucial factor in your giving successful presentations.

Speakers often overlook the reality that the audience is a huge part of every presentation—yes, audiences contribute at least 50% of the communication exchanged. If you think about it, whether it's an audience of one or 10,000, the audience represents at least half of the shared experience.

When you're nervous, it may feel as though you're being observed instead of being a successful transmitter of information to your listeners. When you deliver a presentation, your energy is the vehicle that energizes your listeners. In effect, you're saying, "I'll gladly exchange my knowledge, efforts, and research as a gift for your attention and responsiveness." Audience feedback is critical for improving your delivery.

Your personal appearance on stage matters. When done well, it enhances and simplifies the delivery of your message the same way costumes communicate character qualities for an actor on stage. Appearance helps propel a story forward. If a character comes out on stage dressed in tattered, filthy clothes, the audience recognizes this character as going through a troubled time. The character's appearance communicates an enormous amount of information nonverbally, helping the audience better understand the context for the messages they are about to receive.

In Part II, you'll learn about how to harness and transmit energy for maximum effect to impact audiences, and how to enhance your appearance in ways to inspire your listeners to react to your message in a more meaningful way.

Yes, the audience is crucial.

Chapter 6

Energy

*"You can have all the brainpower in the world
but you have to be able to transmit it.
And the transmission is communication."*

Warren Buffett

Actors and performers learn early on in their training which techniques to use for managing energy. When a performer exudes vibrant energy, the audience feels it and experiences a surge of energy within themselves. Think of the last time you went to a great concert, movie, or speech. That's it. The energy I'm speaking of is different from the "nervous energy" described in Chapter 2. Nervous energy comes from self-consciousness and anxiety; performance energy comes from positive artistic intention and being in the present moment.

For now, accept that we are each of us artists. We, as artists, are conduits of energy that can be harnessed from our environment. When we clarify our intention (see chapter 4) using the techniques I teach, energy flows out through us to our audience. You can learn how to tap into your personal energy as well as the energy available in the room.

I can talk about energy all day long, explain where it comes from and how to make it flow, but I've found that lectures on the subject aren't nearly as effective as clear-cut demonstrations.

In my workshops, I help clients experience the flow of energy to positively impact their listeners. Here are a few ways my methods help my clients.

If you aren't familiar with dancer/choreographer Rudolph Nureyev, watch him perform on YouTube. I saw him dance the Le Corsaire pas de deux during his "Nureyev and Friends" tour. He was electrifying!

During an interview, he said, "I think I'm a very good transmitter. Anything I think or do transmits to the public."

As a performer, YOU are the transmitter of energy. Sharing your energy purposefully with an audience makes the difference between spouting data and delivering an influential message.

I'm predisposed to view presentations through the lens of the theatre. My background is in theatre and the arts; that's the language I speak. Therefore, before I review the how-tos in directing your energy, it will be helpful to clarify some whys for you.

> The most important characteristic of a work of art is unity. The one thing that every work of art has at its center is unity. Unity means harmony among the component parts. What we seek are techniques that will increase the harmony among the component parts.
>
> —William Ball, *A Sense of Direction*

I believe unifying the component parts of the speaker and the audience begins with you. You must unify or harmonize yourself with the audience to transport an effective message.

"How do I know if I'm *unified* with the audience or not?" If you're asking the question, you're ready to learn about the *Second Circle*. Stay with me.

Initially, the goal of my master's thesis was to academically explore what I observed when an actor made a connection with their audience and an observable give and take transpired. After decades of acting and teaching, I crafted my theory of present-moment awareness. But I knew there was something else going on energetically.

My research led to the works of Patsy Rodenburg, OBE, British voice teacher to actors such as Judy Dench, Daniel Craig, and Joseph Fiennes. Rodenburg had done bountiful work supporting the importance of being present. She was curious to learn what made one actor have charisma, the "it" factor, when another lacked it. I agreed with her ideas about leveraging the energetic power in the present moment for the purpose of truly connecting with an audience, successfully delivering *and* receiving information.

In her book *The Second Circle*, Rodenburg distinguished three distinct levels of energetic communication which she explained as three circles of energy. I selected her as one of the seminal sources for my thesis, *The Actor Within: An Exploration of Present-Moment Awareness in Business Presentations.*

Rodenburg briefly explains her three circles as follows (note: they're in non-numerical order for a reason):

> The first circle is where a person withdraws into the self. The opposite is the third circle, the loud and boorish. The second circle is the ideal state, where a person's energy is focused.
>
> It (your energy) moves out towards the object of your attention, touches it then receives energy back from it, you are living on a two-way street—you reach out and touch an energy outside your own, then receive energy back.

The practice of second circle communication techniques to foster better presentations has been instrumental in helping my clients improve their communications. It will be helpful to describe in more detail how you might recognize which circle of energy you are inhabiting.

The Three Circles of Energy

First Circle: The Circle of Self and Withdrawal

Here your whole focus is inward. You can come across to others as self-centered and withdrawn.

You are in First Circle if you:

- Find you are holding your breath
- Find yourself withdrawing physically from people or ideas
- Are asked to repeat yourself when you speak
- Find that people lean forward to hear you
- Feel self-conscious
- Wear clothes that help you to not be noticed

Third Circle: The Circle of Bluff and Force

Your energy is outward moving and untargeted. Your attention is unfocused and lacking precision. You look through people rather than at them. Others may experience you as arrogant, insensitive, and overbearing.

You are in Third Circle if you:

- Notice people withdrawing from you
- Find yourself taking up more space than you need
- Are told often you are too loud in speech or laughter

- Don't notice if people are not enjoying themselves as you are
- Are accused of interrupting others
- Wear clothes that get you noticed

Second Circle: The Energy of Connecting

In the Second Circle, your energy is focused. It moves outward toward your audience, touches it, and receives energy back from it. It's a two-way street of give and take. You are in the present moment—the "zone." In the Second Circle, you are powerful and heard, and leave an impression. The art of being present is the art of operating in the Second Circle.

You know you are in Second Circle if you:
- Feel centered and alert
- Feel your breath is easy and complete
- Feel your body belongs to you
- Notice details in others—their eyes, moods, etc.
- Hear clearly
- Are curious about a new idea
- See, hear, smell, touch something new, which focuses this energy

Actors understand the energy of the Second Circle. It is about communicating, engaging, how you show yourself, how you speak, how you listen.

Now, consider the following techniques to accomplish this goal and unify your energy with that of the audience.

Taking Stage

How many times have you seen a speaker jog up in front of an audience, turn to face everyone, and say, "So. . . "?

"So" what?

So you just undermined the tone of your presentation.

So you missed a significant opportunity to unify with the audience.

So you put the audience on edge without realizing it.

Taking stage with the word "So. . . " is currently one of the most common mistakes businesspeople make giving presentations. Fortunately, it is one of the easiest mistakes to fix.

As a businessperson presenting to a group, you are essentially an actor cast in a role. You would be playing a character who takes the stage in a certain way as defined by the intention and emotion that your character brings. Even when everything on stage is carefully scripted and thought out, things don't always go as planned.

Well-trained actors know how to command a stage in the light of mishaps. It's a honed skill that takes practice and belongs to the fine art of the theatre.

Many of the same theatrical techniques that actors use to manage, control, and respect their audiences at important moments can be successfully applied to business presentations.

What Comes Before

Let's break the process down to its most essential elements. When you are seated and being introduced before your speech, before stepping up to take center stage, you'll want to take your time to prepare. Your presentation process begins before you start speaking. Presenting is not just talking.

Start with a deep breath in. . . and out. This breath will calm you by delivering vital oxygen to your brain. If you're standing in the wings, do the same thing. Ideally, you will find time and privacy to do the complete breathing exercise as described in

Chapter Two. Take several deep breaths in. . . and out and re-state your intention, a process described in Chapter Four.

If you've ever watched Stephen Curry of the Golden State Warriors, you've noticed he takes a deep breath before throwing a free shot. His years of practice have prepared him to get in the present moment.

These actions are *crucial* to transmitting appropriate energy and to the success of your performance.

When you're not prepared and don't perform these steps beforehand, you won't start breathing until after you've spoken the first sentence of your presentation. This is akin to not lacing up your shoes before you go for a run.

Students often say, "Well, my talk wasn't good at the start, but once I got going, I was more comfortable." Their feeling of comfort came because they started breathing! Taking time out to do your deep breathing first will always make the presentation begin more smoothly.

Also, as discussed in Chapter Four, taking deep, measured breaths and recalling your intention is sufficient to calm nerves. This activity will inform your brain that you are safe; the amygdala can settle down and stop sending out danger warning signals. You'll still be feeling excited, as you should be, but you won't be controlled by fear or anxiety if you're prepared.

Coming in with an Ax

An acting teacher told me once to "Come in with an ax." He explained that an actor in sitcoms should enter the scene with the same attention-grabbing energy as "A mother entering the family kitchen carrying an ax!"

If you saw an actor enter a scene wielding an ax, how would you react?

You'd be transfixed.

What's she doing with that ax?

What's going to happen now?

An actor's job is to enter a scene "carrying an ax," grab the audience's attention, and take command of the audience, re-routing their focus to the actor.

But now what would happen if you didn't carry a literal ax, but just pretended to yourself in your own mind that you had one? You would strut on stage carrying a figurative ax, and because of that, you would carry yourself in a certain way. By imagining yourself coming on stage and carrying that ax, you will convey confidence and energy.

How would you apply this to a presentation in a business situation?

You use the same process to take stage.

Don't talk. Take in the entire audience; let your natural energy commandeer the stage.

This informs the audience that you are taking stage.

Here is the process to take stage at a corporate event—without literally carrying an ax!

1. Walk up pleasantly to stand confidently in front of the audience. At that point, you are in the status position. It's a given.
2. Stand with your head and eyes up, taking in the entire room.
3. Draw the audience in with your eyes, from left to right or right to left—whatever feels most comfortable, but always with a pleasant expression.
4. Count in your head: one one thousand, two one thousand, three one thousand, the approximate length of three seconds.

Only after methodically going through these four steps, do you begin speaking.

This process lets the audience know you are present, you are ready, and you are in control. This is the invitation for listeners to unite and connect with you. There is great power and implied authority when using these steps.

There is no "so. . . ," "uhh. . . ," "er. . . ," or "well. . . " uttered by my students.

Taking stage with proper preparation will put you on a smoother path to deliver impactful presentations, and more importantly will put your audience at ease. A polished speaker is like an experienced pilot at the controls of their plane. With authentic confidence, the audience/passengers will instinctively begin to relax.

What goes through your mind when you're about to take stage? Most clients I train say it's usually a jumble of negative emotions.

"What if I fail?"

"What if they see me for the lousy speaker I am?"

"What if it all goes horribly wrong?"

Taking stage with these negative loops running through your mind will make it much harder for you to look and feel confident.

How do you banish such thoughts at a crucial moment? All you need to do is change one simple word: Change "have" into "get."

This means you no longer *have* to give your presentation. You now *get* to give your presentation. You *get* to give your presentation and convey your well-considered intention to an eager audience. Changing that one word changes everything. Now your energy is positively focused and channeled.

It becomes a privilege or an honor to give your presentation, not a chore or a burden.

What do you say to yourself as you're walking up on stage?

"I *get* to give this presentation!"

You no longer dread the experience, you appreciate it.

It's only one little word, but it changes everything.

Michael Kostroff's Golden Rule

The actor Michael Kostroff, best known for his work as defense attorney Maurice Levy in HBO's "The Wire," whom I am also privileged to call my friend, wrote a wonderful book entitled *Audition Psych 101*. In that work, he generously offers readers advice on how to approach casting auditions, an area in which he is a foremost expert. The suggestions he gives actors apply equally well to those doing corporate presentations. Chief among the suggestions is what he calls his Golden Rule:

"Take care of them (your audience). Never ask them to take care of you.

"I'll repeat that. Take care of them. Never ask them to take care of you. You are the doctor; they're the patients. You're the expert; they're the people in need of expertise. Offer something. Ask for nothing."

Having the right mindset is as crucial going into an audition as it is going into a corporate presentation. If your objective is to be well-liked and to receive compliments and encouragement, you will unconsciously place a burden on your audience. Instead, consider what your audience needs and what you can offer. If you provide value, you will be praised and complimented, but those are the byproducts and should not be your purpose.

Take care of them. Never ask them to take care of you. Kostroff's Golden Rule is worth memorizing.

Be Gracious and Be Humble

Now you're on stage, perhaps at a podium wearing a microphone. All eyes are on you. Someone has called you up and introduced you to the waiting crowd. Where do you start?

Being gracious and humble will immediately win favor with your listeners, compared to a speaker who gets up on stage and too eagerly launches into his material.

Thank your audience!

Thank the person who introduced you.

"Thank you for that thoughtful introduction."

"Thank you, Sarah, for organizing this meeting."

"Bob, will you please stand up? Let's give Bob a round of applause for his enormous contribution."

Taking a moment to acknowledge or thank others before starting your prepared remarks gets a presentation off on the right foot. This gives presentations a positive energetic momentum.

Be Prepared

Life is messy. What do you do when you're unexpectedly called up on stage? You have only a few seconds to collect yourself and your thoughts.

How do you keep your mind engaged when you walk up on stage to deliver at your very best, with a minute's notice?

I've been privileged to know some great actors and business people who have handled such improvisational situations with grace and poise. How do they do it?

Actors are human just like the rest of us. At the moment their name is unexpectedly called, they go through the same range of emotions from terror to excitement. The difference is that the calm actors have prepared for these moments with forethought and planning.

Like them, you must decide what your intention is from the moment you step foot in the room until you make your appearance on stage. Ideally, when that happens, you will lose yourself in the moment and not worry about being nervous. You will seek out and find the Second Circle within yourself. Since life is sometimes chaotic, you will need to prepare.

Preparation is the key to releasing that positive energy at the right moment. It starts with your intention. When you are called to make an impromptu speech, your immediate intention should be to show gratitude and graciousness.

Let's suppose you didn't see it coming. You were blindsided when the CEO asked you to come up on stage and say a few words. What then?

Take a deep breath, take two seconds, and think of your intention—it can be compressed to a single word. Whatever else your message may be, if your intention is to express gratitude to your audience, for example, and if you can connect that intention to real emotion as described in Chapter Four, you won't be caught off guard. Instead, you and your audience will become part of two-way energetic communication. You'll be in a mutual collaboration of giving and receiving. Electric!

The emotions you experience as you take stage and as you say your first words will release positive energy. With your intention, connected to a strong feeling and good preparation, the energy you give will come back to you amplified by the audience.

Be Energized

The techniques I've outlined in this chapter, including awareness of the three circles, the concept of unifying yourself with the audience, and focusing on being gracious, can all be used to allow energy to flow through you.

When we're self-conscious as artists, we're blocking our creative energy. The same is true when we're fearful. We're blocking our vitality. When we're not maintaining good eye contact, our energy dissipates like air leaking from a tire.

If you're making presentations and you're not getting positive results, it means your energy is being squandered. If you're not persuading and energizing the audience, it's time to learn how to channel your energy to achieve better results. When you learn the techniques outlined in this chapter, your time and effort will pay off with moving and influential presentations.

When a presenter and an audience align in unity, it's pure magic!

Chapter 7

Appearance

"It's not about having money. If you have a suit that cost $150, go the extra mile and get it tailored. Shine your shoes. Make sure you manicure your nails. It's the simple things that people notice, that take you far."

Daymond John

When presenting, you are judged on your appearance: the clothes you wear, your hairstyle, your shoes, and even your manicure. You're the speaker. More than that, the clothes you wear affect how you feel in your body. Consequently, you will move differently in workout clothes than you would in a suit for a formal gathering. Your clothes directly influence your feelings, behavior, and the way you are perceived by the audience. Your appearance matters.

Imagine yourself as an actor playing a role. Actors understand the critical nature of each costume. A well-designed, well-made costume and "look" enhance characterization while providing strong visual support of the story, concept, and context of the play. There are many costume discussions and fittings to get it right. And it's fun to get it right!

When making an important business presentation, you need to give your image more than a passing thought. To get it right, you may need to make a significant investment.

The advice I give my clients who are prepping for a high-stakes presentation is to "bump it up one." What does that mean? If everyone in the office dresses in t-shirts and jeans, as the presenter you are in the status position. You should go for nicer jeans and a polo shirt with a collar.

Bumping it up one usually means that if you are presenting to people who are dressed business casual, you need to wear nicer shoes and nicer casual attire than your audience. Aim to go one notch higher, but not significantly more formal.

I was brought in to coach a senior VP of security in a major tech company who was up for promotion. Wendy was perhaps the most beautiful woman I have ever seen—which is saying a lot. Acting attracts the gorgeous specimens among us, and I've coached dozens of women who were tens on anyone's scale, but Wendy was drop dead gorgeous.

It turned out that being too alluring was a serious problem for Wendy. She looked so sexy in typical business casual out-fits it was distracting.

The advice I gave her: dress down! I suggested that she wear tailored, conservative clothes that didn't have sex appeal (no sleeveless tops, no tight jeans or sweaters), and to wear min-imal makeup. In that state, she easily bumped it up one com-pared to her audience. She was still eye-catching and attrac-tive, but not a distraction to her presentation.

Ironically, after we completed our work together, Wendy re-ceived the prestigious CSO Magazine and Women of Influence award, "*One to Watch!*" She developed into a community leader and was promoted numerous times. Winning the award recognized her education, intelligence, hard work, and the new leadership and communication techniques I taught her.

Like Wendy, you need to give your appearance serious focus and consideration. Hairstylists, makeup artists, manicurists, and clothing consultants are important resources if you want to make your best impression.

I often encourage my clients not to scrimp. The right outfit put together smartly will not only give you an emotional boost; it will help your audience feel more positively towards you. After all, we dress out of respect for our audience.

If they notice that your shoes are scruffy, your jacket doesn't fit right, or your hair is a mess, they will be focused on those things while you're hoping they're getting your message.

Another brilliant student I coached, Marguerite, spoke English as a third language. She worked as a mid-level manager in a medical firm and was referred to me by her boss who saw her potential and wanted to help her move forward in her career.

Marguerite and I worked together one on one for three months, one to two sessions every week. I saw a spectacular improvement over that period. At first, she spoke with her head and eyes down, so softly I could barely hear her. Her English was excellent but she didn't know how to convey information effectively to her audience. She also dressed carelessly and without any style. She needed well-tailored dress shirts, quality shoes, and time to focus on what looked good on her petite frame.

To her credit, Marguerite was an amazingly hard worker who was willing to take direction. She told me she spent twenty solid hours outside of our sessions working on the exercises I gave her. She took all my advice to heart. When it came to her appearance, she was all in. She invested in new wardrobe pieces and spent serious dollars on hair, makeup, and nails. It was worth every penny.

Marguerite's presentations began to get attention, and her colleagues noticed that not only was she smart and articulate, but she also presented a great image of their company to clients. A few months after working with her, I was thrilled to receive a call from her boss: Marguerite was promoted!

When it comes to improving your presentations, clothing and appearance can be the easiest things to fix. Unlike other aspects of public speaking, you can simply invest time and money to fix many a glaring weakness. And, it can be fun!

You'll discover your "list of friends" will increase. The more knowledge and experience you gain, chances are the more you will be called upon to share it with others. That will lead to more presenting! In turn, more presenting will lead to more clothes, better haircuts, well-maintained shoes. . . It's a virtuous cycle.

You need to find the time to take care of yourself. Early on in our careers, professional actors learn how valuable their team of friends can become. Take the time to care for how you look and feel. Manage your time. Don't let time manage you.

If needed, I always suggest you put together a great team to support your efforts. All of the advice below applies to everyone.

Hairstylist: You must find a stylist who knows how to cut your hair type. Thin, fine, straight hair requires a different cut than a cut for thick and/or curly hair.

Cobbler: Invest in well-made, comfortable shoes and get them re-heeled and polished. You'll save a fortune on shoes and look great.

Manicurist: People notice your nails, so your nails must be immaculate and well-shaped. A good manicure doesn't need to be painful to be well done. And a good pedicure is worth the time and money.

Tailor: Do you have short arms or legs, narrow shoulders, a wider waist? You'll need a good tailor. Your tailor must have a great eye, give honest feedback on how a piece fits your body, and use careful stitches.

Massage Therapist: If you're feeling tension in your neck, shoulders, or back, don't ignore it. A good L.M.T. (licensed massage therapist) or C.M.P. (certified massage practitioner) can alleviate stress that could diminish your performance. Take care of yourself first so you can better care for your audience.

Esthetician: A good facial is worth its weight in gold. There's a reason why actors look great!

Makeup Artist: I recommend the Bobby Brown counter at Nordstrom to start. Their advisors are helpful. You don't need to pile on the makeup, but you do want your face to be the major focus. If you don't usually wear any makeup, even a little blush and lipstick informs the audience where to look. Many professional women I coach believe that makeup is unnecessary, but that's a mistake. Excellent makeup will greatly enhance your features, and when done properly can make you look amazing.

Because we are all different, and because how we carry ourselves in clothes varies, the work you and I do together building your look is always very individual. But I will offer some general advice about the clothes and grooming you'll need if you want to present your very best self.

If you want to learn more about looking your best for business presentations, I highly recommend you read any of the classic books on the subject that you'll find on Amazon such as *New Women's Dress for Success*, by John T. Molloy,

Dressing the Man, by Alan Flusser, or *How to Get Dressed,* by Alison Freer.

If you don't have time to read and study an entire book on the subject, here is a link to a helpful infographic that summarizes many of the key ideas about how to dress for a business meeting: https://www.entrepreneur.com/article/238953.

When it comes to making good wardrobe and appearance choices, any such books will be helpful. Remember, your goal is to cast yourself in a favorable light while avoiding the pitfall of looking either too dressy or too casual. You want your audience to recall only that you were well-dressed, not to remember anything specific about your appearance!

To achieve that objective, my single most important piece of advice is this: take time to look and feel your best before you step in front of an audience. The practice and preparation you do to deliver an amazing presentation are easily lost if you look stressed or aren't dressed appropriately. On the flip side, the investments you make in your appearance will always pay handsome dividends.

Part III

Your Message

Preface to Part III

The way to craft a successful story hasn't changed much since Aristotle 2400 years ago. If actors, directors, and writers could have improved his methods and made them easier, we would have done so already.

Your story, your message always starts with an idea, long before you craft your presentation. When you finally have your finished presentation, then you're ready to rehearse the delivery. I guarantee obstacles are going to surface. In Part III, I will guide you through the processes to alleviate those obstacles and take you through the steps to a polished presentation.

By the end of your reading, you may be surprised to learn that you have gained an appreciation of how pivotal collaboration is in all of your relationships—call it the cherry on the top! It's the gift that comes from a well-communicated message, perceptive listening, and influential delivery.

With my guidance for honest self-evaluation, your commitment to dig down deep and pay attention to audience cues, you will experience the pleasure of working collaboratively. Collaborating with others isn't just talking to people; it's a creative communication process that develops into the most sophisticated manner to interact with others.

Chapter 8

Idea

"What lies behind us and what lies before us are tiny matters, compared to what lies within us. And when we bring what is within out into the world, miracles happen."

Ralph Waldo Emerson

I've learned everyone has something interesting to say. Every presentation skills workshop I've facilitated has proven it. Sometimes people have a hard time expressing their ideas, especially in a group setting. Fear can get in the way of voicing original thoughts.

My clients ask me how they can get past their nerves and fear to the source of ideas around which to wrap their presentation. In response, I tell them I've developed a system to get them through that knothole of fear and from there, creativity will flow.

"I'm afraid that when I stand in front of the audience, I'll forget everything and my mind will go blank," said Britney, a petite systems engineer who attended one of my workshops.

If I had a dime for every time I've had a client tell me this. . .

Consider that an average human brain has 100 billion nerve cells, each connected to as many as 10,000 other neurons. If you do the math, it means there are up to 1000 trillion synaptic connections in the brain. That means is that you never need to worry about running out of thoughts, ideas, memories, or words. We all have plenty of capacity.

So why does Britney's mind go blank when she stands in front of an audience? The simple answer is fear.

Fortunately, when you override situational fear, ideas will immediately surface.

One of the techniques I use to eliminate fear from blocking creativity is having my workshop students play specific improvisational games. These games are specific to the components of my system: Body, Voice, Intention, and Improvisation.

"Oh, you mean like we're going to do improv comedy?" Britney asks.

"Well, sort of," I reply. "We're going to start with an exercise I experienced in workshops lead by the great actor and teacher Alan Arkin. Alan's wife Suzanne is a psychotherapist, and together they teach improvisation as a life skill, not just a skill used in performance. Alan shows how to use improvisation to tap into an unlimited source of creative energy. Once you learn how to access that place in yourself, you'll be able to return there whenever you choose. The best way to understand this technique is to experience it."

I ask everyone to form a circle. I reach down to the floor and pick up an imaginary tennis ball. "Can you all see the ball?" I say, holding the ball up to show them.

They nod yes.

"Great! You're all delusional!"

I toss the imaginary tennis ball over to Britney, who catches it and, following instructions, pretends to throw it to another workshop attendee. The newness of this experience, the awkwardness of doing this pretend thing that's out of her comfort zone, results in her trying to be clever and funny. A few people nervously laugh. You know, those forced, inauthentic laughs. Following Britney's lead, others try silly actions in attempts to be funny.

I let their self-imposed demand to be funny continue a bit longer. "Human beings are intrinsically creative," I say. "We don't have to try to be creative. There's no need to act funny or anything else. Let's simply keep the ball moving."

In this exercise, it takes participants several minutes before reaching a deeper understanding of what's happening. Eventually, they settle into a pattern of not trying to be funny, or creative, or throwing the ball in a different and original way. They simply fall into a natural place and authentically go with the flow. Each toss and catch is executed while the player is present in that moment.

What happens next always thrills me. Participants begin to focus their attention *and* intention on the tennis ball: the size of the ball, the speed of the ball, the direction it is coming at them from, where and to whom they throw, taking care each catcher sees it and catches it successfully. A sincere give and take takes place.

At this point, real creativity spontaneously occurs. Genuinely funny and clever things start to happen—not a contrived comedy, but authentic reactions and feelings. The goal is not to be funny. The goal is to experience the feeling of being in the present moment with focus.

That's exactly what happened in this workshop. Britney got offended when someone threw the ball at her too hard, and people laughed because her reaction was honest and so real. She wasn't trying to be funny, but she was. In that present moment, the ball speed was unexpected and she got miffed. Another participant held the ball as carefully as a baby chick, handing it over to the woman next to him. She accepted it with gentle pats.

Here is why the exercise works. Focusing on the tennis ball, or any object, allows a person's idea (their intention) to replace their fears and stress. Students relax into the task of throwing an imaginary tennis ball and feel the source of their natural creativity and personal originality.

This simple exercise loosens us up and allows anyone to tap into a wellspring of creativity. Having permission to "do nothing" encourages creativity to surface and thrive. When we stop trying so hard and being disingenuous, we move out of fear to a place where ideas germinate and come to life. We can't stop them from coming.

You may be wondering how this translates into delivering a more expressive presentation. The process is twofold: It starts with having a clear intention, i.e., the message you are delivering in the moment. Recall in earlier chapters you've read how it's critical to find your intention before you speak. The second part is connecting your intention (your idea) to a strong feeling. Feelings are accessible inside you—sometimes deep within, so you may need time to reflect first to gain awareness and articulate your specific feeling. Taking deep breaths will help you connect to your feelings.

I've been helping workers at tech companies in Silicon Valley for nearly twenty years, and I will tell you the concept of getting an idea and connecting it to emotion is crucial. The process can be challenging work for tech people! Many have a disconnect between their analytical thoughts and emotional terrain. That's why the exercises I've shared in this book are so important. The exercises will help you bypass fear, get clear on your ideas, connect to an emotion, express intention, and deliver all that with energy. It will take practice. However, my experience shows that everyone has this ability. Great actors have known all this for many decades.

Intention and Emotion

You may have heard of Konstantin Stanislavski, or no doubt you've heard of method acting. Many of the world's greatest actors continue to use his method to create riveting performances on stage and screen. Over the last eighty years, the shorthand "What's my motivation?" has become the CliffsNotes version of method acting. Intention and motivation don't mean exactly the same thing, but they're very close cousins.

If you want to see an arresting performance, watch the opening scene from the movie *My Left Foot* about the Irish poet and artist Christy Brown, portrayed by Daniel Day-Lewis. The movie was nominated for five Academy Awards and won two including best actor for Day-Lewis. During the filming of the production, he remained in character the whole time he was on set and required the crew to carry him and spoon feed him. In that opening scene, we watch him put a record on a turntable using just his left foot, a task he took on because he was told it was impossible.

His director in that film, Jim Sheridan, was quoted as saying that Day-Lewis "hates acting" because he rejects the idea that he would act out an emotion or moment. His objective in every film is to embody the character and to be thoroughly immersed in every detail of that character's life and personality. In preparation for that opening scene of "My Left Foot," for example, he spent weeks practicing putting the toner arm needle on the record and spent another eight weeks with cerebral palsy patients.

Few people will ever rise to the performance heights achieved by Daniel Day-Lewis, but what we can learn from him is that meticulous preparation to every minute detail produces riveting results.

You may be thinking, "But, I'm not an actor! I'm a business-person who has company information to deliver."

You don't need to learn the Stanislavski method but you do need to understand that before you step out on stage, you must firmly establish your intention, and then you must connect that intention to an emotion.

What does it mean to connect an intention to an emotion? The following will help you understand how to do that when you're delivering your presentation.

Delivery Preparation

The delivery of your presentation is the final step in my workshops. I don't disclose that information prematurely because students aren't adequately prepared until they've worked through the system and sequence of training exercises. In my experience, most people have to work harder than they expected to connect to a strong feeling. They need to identify an emotion and connect that emotion to their intention, i.e., what they intend to communicate.

Here is a common excuse I hear at every company seminar I teach: "I'm just given preprepared slides and I have to deliver the presentation next week to a group of colleagues. The presentation is given to me, and there's no room for putting my own spin on it."

I say to them, "If that presentation doesn't ignite something in you, and get you to feel strongly about some aspect of it, give it to somebody else to deliver."

And they reply, "Well, I can't. I can't do that. I'm the one who has to give the presentation."

"Well, in that case, it's your responsibility as the presenter, as the speaker, to find something in that presentation that you *do* feel strongly about—it can be pro or con—but there must be something."

For an audience to receive value during your presentation, there must be an emotional exchange in the ideas shared. The presenter needs to communicate a sincerity about something, whether it's numbers or facts shown on a graph or the company's loss or gain.

It is the presenter's responsibility to find something that he or she feels strongly about in that presentation. If not, send everyone an email and save them from the torture of listening to a presentation with no emotion-filled content! I'm serious.

For an idea, or an intention to work, it *must* be connected to a strong feeling.

Where Do Ideas Come From?

I don't know!

Alan Arkin said in his memoir *An Improvised Life* that all of life is an improvisation, whether you like it or not.

> That's what we're all doing, all the time, whether we know it or not. Whether we like it or not. Creating something on the spur of the moment with the materials at hand. We might just as well let the rest of it go, join the party, and dance our hearts out.

Los Angeles artist Mark Bradford, who was featured in an interview with Anderson Cooper on "60 Minutes" is a good example of how breakthrough ideas can happen by accident.*

Broke and struggling, Mark Bradford couldn't afford expensive paints for creating art. He got an idea one day that transformed his career direction. Working in his mother's hair salon, he noticed some endpapers used for styling hair on the floor. It occurred to him he could use those endpapers to make a design. In an instant, his mind shifted to seeing the translucent papers in a new way, like art materials. Thus began three decades of making large scale "paintings" that use little or no paint, but inexpensive paper and other materials found in hardware stores. Trusting his instincts, this breakthrough moment changed the course of his life.

That accident launched Bradford's career and turned him into one of the most successful artists of our day. His work is so original that you can't take your eyes off it. When you watch him work, you can see that he is an improvisation in action. He tears, he rips, he sands, and somehow his creative idea takes shape.

When you have a presentation to deliver on a particular subject, you need to harness your personal creative and energetic flow. When you can accomplish that, you're golden!

Turning an idea into a vibrant presentation will always be hard work, but working without a creative spark will be agonizing.

The difference is talking in front of people feeling self-conscious, nervous, and judged, or having the satisfaction and joy of helping to educate people, which pulls honest emotional connection and energy from your audience.

---

* Here's a link to the interview: https://www.cbsnews.com/news/artist-mark-bradford-the-60-minutes-interview-2019-05-12/)

Presentations that resonate with audiences don't just parse out information. Good presentations educate and inspire an audience so listeners spark to what's inside them. When you make this emotional connection, your message has been received.

Going for the Gold

When it comes to the point in a training seminar when I am ready to assign participants the task of crafting a presentation, the only stipulation given is that the topic has to be something the participant cares about. The subject can be anything—cutting roses, making cabbage soup, raising chickens—literally anything. Speakers then have the two legs to solidify their delivery: Intention (what they're speaking about) and its connection to an emotion (strong feeling).

Everyone has something interesting to say.

Over the years, I've heard some unusual and off-beat presentations. One participant, a hardware engineer, brought a boom tube (exhaust pipe) into the workshop. He designed and built it himself. His hobby was racing cars. Another participant spoke at length about peanut butter. A young woman chose to talk about ballet. A former American Ballet Theatre company member, she demonstrated a développé, elegantly lifting her leg all the way up, toes pointing, past her ear!

Lest you think interesting presentations need only be about unusual personal subjects: I worked with ten engineers at Lockheed Martin years ago. One shy ESL scientist began telling us about the Mars landing module design he had worked on. His presentation was sounding like gibberish to me. I stopped him and instructed him to take a moment and connect to a strong feeling he had about what he wanted us to understand. He took that moment, inhaled deeply, exhaled, and began his presentation again. It was riveting. I understood every word. I got excited to learn more. His fellows gave him a round of applause so heartfelt that he couldn't hold back his smile.

These were compelling presentations. Why? Because each presenter was individually ignited; they cared deeply about their subjects. Their intention was connected to a strong emotion. I've also had students who were passionate about a topic but didn't know how to turn their emotions into a meaningful presentation.

Occasionally, presenters have too much undirected emotion that can become problematic for expressing well-thought-out ideas. In recent years I've been hired by companies dealing with groups of employees expressing a range of grievances including sexual harassment, unfavorable working conditions, and a host of diversity issues. To be effective, those unsettled employees needed to learn how to channel negative feelings into useful, focused, and directed presentations for management consideration. In workshops such as these, I have used the same techniques I've laid out here; the same principles apply.

However, in those cases, we worked in the opposite direction. We started by getting clear on the negative emotions first, then worked to channel those emotions with ideas for change. That combination gave my participants the tools to develop self-empowerment. That process helped them to find their voices and ultimately connect to their ideas and deliver clear and effective messages in their presentations, ultimately improving the company cultures. Several ERG (employee resource groups) have been established in the larger companies I have helped.

I have to tell ya, I don't know where ideas come from. But I do know my system works to get connected to how you feel about them and communicate them well.

And Britney, the systems engineer? She went through my training program with flying colors. Despite her initial skepticism—that I encouraged and appreciated!—she learned that the methods I taught her allowed her to override her fears, tap into a wellspring of ideas, connect her ideas to a strong feeling, and use that combination to deliver excellent presentations. Yes, it required real training, practice, and effort, but when I last checked in with her, she reported that the process of creating presentations had gotten faster and easier. And like so many of my students, her improved presentation skills had side benefits, not just in business but in life.

Finding her voice allowed Britney to relax when presenting, more confidently ask for what she needed, and, overall, discover more satisfaction in her relationships, life, and career. There's nothing more gratifying for me to hear than that!

Chapter 9

Presentation

"If you don't know what you want to achieve in your presentation, your audience never will."

Harvey Diamond

As a young actress, I ran with a talented group. Many continued on to have successful careers in acting and the arts. Occasionally, one of my cohorts would direct a play. If they encountered trouble with a scene or two, I found myself invited to sit in on a rehearsal and take notes. I seemed to have an ability to recognize what was working and what wasn't, what was funny and what wasn't. And (because I have been inclined to express my opinions readily since I was three years old) I would suggest ideas on how to fix the problematic areas. The scenes improved. Now I make my living as a *play doctor* of sorts for business presentations.

When it comes to presentations, I do not offer one-size-fits-all instructions. My specialized contribution as the *presentation doctor* is to work with you to hone your style, your story, your edits, and focus on your successful delivery. My value add is to diagnose what's working and to correct what isn't. Not surprisingly, your presentations improve.

Rather than a how-to on creating presentations, this chapter is a broad-brushstroke overview of how to think differently about your approach to presenting—how you craft and deliver your presentations. It includes some of the major pitfalls and general advice I offer on presentations.

This may come as a surprise. I don't spend a lot of class time instructing clients in great detail on HOW to write a presentation. If that type of guidance is needed, anyone can find a good book, or Google "how to build a business presentation" and find lots of useful articles and videos.

What I do go over is the basic presentation format. Students return to do their presentation after they write the content. Then, like the processes discussed throughout this book, we work collaboratively, preparing from the inside out, crafting and polishing the presentation.

In my workshops, I provide students with a course workbook containing the six steps I recommend to keep in mind when building their presentation. They are:

Step 1: Who is Your Audience? The more specific the better.

Step 2: What Is Your Intention? (See Chapter 4—Your Intention.) Do not step onto any stage until you have a clear understanding of your intention and have connected it to a strong feeling.

Step 3: What Goes in the Body of Your Presentation? Cut to the chase: Tell the STORY! Is it interesting? Is it informative? Is it useful? If you can't answer those questions with a "Heck, yeah!" then you're not digging deep enough inside yourself.

Step 4: How Will You Connect It All? People forget about incorporating segues, and they're critical to presentations. A useful resource for segues and transitions comes from the Royal Melbourne Institute of Technology (RMIT) in Australia which published a two-page guide to using signaling and transition words in oral presentations.* You'll find helpful segue suggestions.

Step 5: How Will You Open? How will you introduce yourself? How will you get your audience's attention? How will you describe your topic?

Step 6: How Will You Close? Your close consists of:

- A brief summary: "In summary. . . "
- Q&A: "This may have raised some questions for you. . ."
- One sentence with the final message: "The one idea I want you to remember is. . . "

Your Visuals

At last, we come to the slides!

Slides are boring. There. I said it. *You* are much more interesting than slides.

Sometimes I get a panicked call from a former student asking for help with their presentation slides.

"Billie, I'm never going to get through fifty slides in ten minutes. What the heck am I supposed to do?"

I'm going to give you the same advice I give them:

Don't start with the slides!

That may sound like counterintuitive advice, but it's not. Slides are meant to supplement your talk. Slides are there to support you, not the other way around! You are not beholden to the slides. Focusing on the slides first can limit your creativity when crafting your presentation.

Everybody knows that, right?

---

* Oral Presentations: Signaling and Transition Words, RMIT University Study and Learning Centre, 2014. (https://emedia.rmit.edu.au/learninglab/sites/default/files/Oral_presentations_signalling_2014_Accessible.pdf)

Unfortunately not. When I begin to work with people one on one, they always start with the slides. I say, "Don't start with the slides." Then they come in with their slides all prepared, expecting everything will follow from that.

Go read an entire book on visual aids and presentation graphics if you want, but here is a simple overview, borrowing heavily from some standard, useful sources.

When using slides, I suggest as a base point following the tried and true Guy Kawasaki Rule: 10-20-30. That means no more than ten slides, no more than twenty minutes, and a font no smaller than thirty point.*

I also recommend reading the classic *Presentation Zen* by Garr Reynolds. It offers an enlightened approach to showing slides. "Less is more" applies here.

When it comes to communicating visually, here are two key ideas to keep in mind, adapted from Jerry Weissman's *Presenting to Win*.

Question 1: Why don't your graphics work?
- Are they too cluttered?
- Are they too detailed?
- Is the print too small?
- Is your slide a data dump?

Question 2: Do your slides support your presentation?
- Do they add focus to the presentation?
- Do they minimize eye sweeps?
- Do they summarize key information in a "less is more" way?

If you want a deep dive into creating presentations, do read Weissman's book.

---

* https://guykawasaki.com/the-only-10-slides-you-need-in-your-pitch/

How to Prepare a 5-Minute Presentation

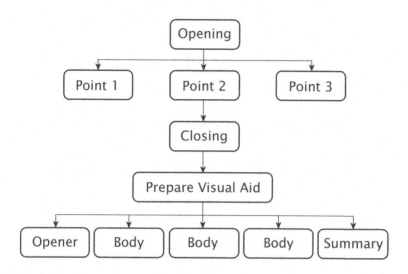

A Five-Minute Presentation

Sometimes they won't come to you on Tuesday and tell you to make a presentation on Thursday. Instead, they'll come to you at 11:00 AM and tell you you're going on stage at 11:15 AM! With almost no prep time, you'll have to get up and deliver a five-minute presentation. To accomplish the task, I recommend you use many of the same techniques described in this chapter, but I've distilled it further to the essentials:

Six Common Presentation Mistakes

Take a moment to review (and avoid) these six mistakes I have observed speakers commonly make when delivering presentations.

1. UNCLEAR THINKING If you can't explain your topic in less than two minutes, you don't understand it.

2. NO CLEAR STRUCTURE Don't waffle or ramble. You'll lose your listeners.
3. TALKING TOO MUCH Silence and sound have equal value.
4. NO MEMORABLE STORIES People remember the images your story inspired.
5. NO EMOTIONAL CONNECTION Your edge is creating emotional connections with your audience.
6. NOT ENOUGH REHEARSAL Time it! If you go over your allotted time, you could be stealing time from the next speaker.

On to the Final Steps

Two people can deliver the *exact* same presentation, word for word, and while one soars, another bombs. What's the difference? It's in the delivery.

Once you've got your clear and concise presentation together, you're *almost* at the finish line. Before you take the final step of delivering your polished presentation, there could be a few hurdles coming. In the next chapter, we'll take a closer look at some of the more common obstacles that could get in the way of putting your best self forward.

Chapter 10

Rehearsal

*"It usually takes more than three weeks to
prepare a good impromptu speech."*

Mark Twain

You imagine yourself electrifying your audience with a dazzling presentation.

You see yourself smiling and taking bows in front of an appreciative crowd. They loved it! You were awesome! By all accounts, it was an inspiring appearance.

Your question is "How do I get from where I am to a dazzling, inspiring presentation?"

Here is your answer: deliberate practice.

Note that practice and deliberate practice are two different things. "Deliberate" is the operative word.

A note about operative words: Operative words are a vital tool for actors. Basically, they are the most important words in the script and help get the meaning across to the audience. You want to be aware of the operative words in important phrases within your presentation.

You might sit down to practice the piano every day for an hour, playing the same pieces in the same way, for years, and never get better! Hundreds of hours spent making the same mistakes are not the same as hundreds of hours spent carefully analyzing your weaknesses and methodically practicing and improving each time.

One approach is mechanical and the other involves constant inquiry, feedback, and adjustment.

No one shows up on a Broadway stage without having put in thousands of hours of deliberate practice—training, going to classes, acting workshops, working one on one with a coach or mentor who evaluates, sculpts, and expands their skill set.

Certain people may be more "gifted" or not, but the only point worth debating is whether you will commit yourself and focus to become an awesome presenter. I can give you all the tools, tips, tricks, techniques, and tactics, but just reading this book, or any number of books, simply won't be sufficient.

I am still shocked that senior managers and executives can spend hours crafting emails yet balk at the idea of investing hours practicing their presentations!

Let's say you spend thirty minutes rehearsing your fifteen-minute presentation. You run through it twice. Would you have a reasonable expectation of it being okay? I'm not talking about being great. I'm asking whether you will even be okay.

That's a NO—a hard NO.

You want to be confident, comfortable, and certain when you stand in front of your audience, but you might not realize you need to set aside time for structured rehearsal.

Here are some of the benefits when you focus on your presentation skills and rehearse.

- You improve your delivery
- You clarify the operative words in your message
- You solidify your opening and closing

- You clean up transitions from subject to subject
- You improve your message
- You decrease anxiety and calm your fears
- You make discoveries about yourself and the presentation
- You improve your timing so you speak concisely and coherently
- You enjoy making presentations because you're helping others when you deliver helpful information

Ideally, if you want to deliver a dynamic fifteen-minute performance, you will need to rehearse a minimum of five hours.

Can you rehearse by yourself? Yes, and you definitely should. That said, the only way to get significantly better is to receive feedback. It can be helpful to videotape yourself. You may be able to analyze some of your mistakes, but can you review your performance in an objective, trained way? If you're without a presentation coach, at the very least ask someone trustworthy to give you candid, objective critique.

When Actors Rehearse

Rehearsal is crucial to every theatrical performance. The rehearsal rules for actors in an Equity production can be complicated and varied. To simplify: You may not realize that professional actors rehearse five to six days a week, eight to ten hours per day, for four to five weeks, depending. And each day, after rehearsal, actors usually go home, study the script, and deliberately practice some more.

Why is this so important? The discoveries that are uncovered during rehearsals are the creative and thrilling miracles of acting. It may sound like a huge amount of preparation, which it is, but rehearsals are also some of the most joyful parts of being an actor.

When I coach corporate executives and managers, the first thing I tell them is that rehearsals, when done correctly, will be fun and exciting. Of course, it will involve concentration, focus, attention, and dedication. This may sound like work, but there aren't many more joyful experiences in life than being fully present and in the moment, which is what rehearsals teach you. Rehearsals should be fun, and when done correctly, you'll have a new appreciation for your own skills, style, and abilities.

Over the past decades, I've worked with some senior executives of large companies who don't fully appreciate the need to prioritize rehearsal time. They're busy, of course, but occasionally they think that hiring me will immediately transform them into amazing presenters. I wish it were that easy!

Rehearsal, whether you're an actor or a businessperson, is a collaborative process during which a coach offers constructive feedback and explains what adjustments need to be made mentally and physically to achieve a better outcome. What could be more important?

Steve Jobs: Deliberate Presenter

In case you didn't know, Steve Jobs, the legendary CEO of Apple, prioritized his presentations above all else. Why? Jobs knew that to inspire people to follow his lead or buy his products, he needed to be staggeringly good on stage. And he was. His presentations are one of the many things for which Jobs is best remembered.

Here's a quote from an interview with Brent Schlender, author of *Becoming Steve Jobs*:

Steve spent months preparing for his product intros and other public appearances and rehearsed them exhaustively. I once spent an entire day watching him run through multiple rehearsals of a single presentation, tweaking everything from the color and angle of certain spotlights, to editing and rearranging the order of the keynote presentation slides to improve his pacing. He could get pretty petulant if some technical aspect went awry. In one instance that day, he just sat silently on stage with his chin in his hand, staring at the floor for nearly fifteen minutes, out of frustration with a wrong lighting cue. He didn't yell this time, but just made everyone wait while he cooled down. Even before that stage, he would call journalists like me or Steven Levy who wrote for *Newsweek* and later *Wired,* to try out metaphors and lines he was thinking about using, just to see if we thought they resonated. This could be weeks and weeks before the actual event.

Jobs practiced and rehearsed so much because he valued himself. He "gave himself the oxygen on the airplane first" so that he could then give to others.

The president of a Silicon Valley software company hired me to help him with a major presentation he was to deliver at an international Asia-Pacific Economic Cooperative summit. He learned shortly before his presentation that he was scheduled to appear on stage in a lineup that included Jack Ma, the CEO of Alibaba, a dynamic speaker.

He could have felt a little intimidated. He realized he needed my coaching expertise. We spent nearly twelve hours that week in one-on-one rehearsal time. Together we clarified his intention and crafted a dynamic story. He put in hours deliberately practicing the adjustments I gave him, refining his diction, blocking, vocal modulation, and timing. His presentation was awesome. In the end, it didn't matter who spoke before or after him at the conference because he delivered the best version of himself and his company. Was it overkill to spend that much time? Absolutely not. We refined and polished, and each time the presentation got better.

If you want to deliver dynamic presentations, if you want your words to have an impact, if you want to inspire, lead, or sell, you *must* be willing to invest the time in yourself, just like Steve Jobs. Public speaking is a deliberately practiced skill that you cannot outsource or delegate.

Throughout this book, there are exercises and techniques for improving your presentations, all of which take time and effort. Know that the time you invest in this deliberate practice will benefit you greatly. When done correctly with focus and intention, the process will be creative and fun.

Discovering your best self and your onstage persona is also incredibly gratifying and may inspire you in ways you never imagined possible.

Chapter 11

Obstacles

*"The single biggest problem in communication
is the illusion that it has taken place."*

George Bernard Shaw

At the start of each new class, I ask the question "How many people here get nervous or scared before they make a presentation? Raise your hand." Sometimes people half-raise their hands. Most times people don't raise their hands at all. Why? Because they're too scared to admit that they're scared!

Our brains are wired the same way. There's little chance the amygdala will let us get away without feeling nervous or afraid before facing an audience. It's the job of our temporal lobe amygdala to warn us when it perceives danger approaching. Professional actors are no different than the rest of us—we get just as nervous and have the same fear responses before performances. You're going to feel nervous!

The difference between trained actors and untrained business speakers is that actors have learned techniques to redirect that nervous energy into a positive intention, or objective.

Because everyone experiences being nervous, we develop techniques—coping mechanisms—over the years to help us manage stressful experiences.

The tactics we all employ to circumvent or cope with emotionally charged situations served us when we adopted them. An embarrassing situation in the fourth grade may still be in subconscious operation. A humiliating circumstance in college can still be impacting our responses at work or in our relationships.

By the time a new client is face to face with me, I spot their obstacles to success immediately. My clients are accomplished and they excel in their chosen fields, but what they lack are the necessary refinements to any outdated strategies they continue to use. It's like that old adage—if you only have a hammer in your tool kit, then you solve all your problems as if they were nails.

To help my students understand the behaviors that have become obstacles, I've made a list of the most common ones. I've touched on some of these in previous chapters where I have included simple solutions. When these solutions are practiced, it's possible to recognize your improvement in short order.

You have to know what it feels like when you are interjecting "um" or "uhh" while presenting to an audience, and then experience how it feels when you are not using them. Once you practice it, you'll be on the road. It's not easy but it's not complicated.

When you become aware of the particular obstacles getting in the way of your presentations and performances, you'll recognize when you're using an old habit. Thankfully, it won't feel "right" or comfortable anymore. You will have a new technique to replace those obsolete habits. Productive communication is the result of implementing the strategies I teach. Here are a few examples.

Likeability

When a client is in front of an audience delivering information, I like to have them think about that situation from the perspective of playing a role in a stage play. Let's say that as an actor, the role you've been hired to play is a competent speaker or a powerful leader.

If you're cast in my play and you're playing the role of a competent speaker, there are certain character qualities that are embodied in that character. Among the most valuable qualities is likeability. What are the qualities of likeability?

The list includes:

- An appropriate smile
- Conveying appropriate energy
- Being good-natured rather than arrogant or negative
- Having the ability to laugh at oneself without being too self-effacing if you make a mistake (It's not how we fall; it's how we get up.)
- Sharing personal experiences that are authentic
- The ability to have a good time—enjoying sharing information and helping people
- To care about and be interested in the subject
- A friendly tone of voice

Likeability is an important attribute to cultivate and project to your audience when delivering a presentation to an audience of one or 1000. (You may recall the Second Circle benefits from Chapter 6—Your Energy.) Listeners tend to forgive less-than-stellar performances when they like the speaker. Arrogant, know-it-all, or robotic speakers don't understand the value of audience connection.

Speaker Confidence

Just as there are qualities that go into a character to show like-ability, there are other qualities that demonstrate confidence. When speakers get on stage and pace back and forth, they may believe nervous energy helps them think, but audiences view such behavior as low self-confidence. The same goes for leaning forward and stepping backward.

Pausing during presentations is a great way to demonstrate speaker confidence. It's important to recognize that silence and sound have equal value. Confident individuals don't need to rush to the next phrase or sentence. They feel secure enough to express a thought, stop for a beat, and then express another thought. This allows the intended information to "land" with the audience, allowing them to play a part in the presentation experience. This tells the listener "I'm here for you. There's no place I would rather be. I'm not in a hurry because you are my priority."

Good posture, concise wording, speaking with certainty, keeping the head still—these are all signs of high confidence (see the chart on the next page.) With practice and honest feedback from a coach, it's possible to go from delivering presentations with low confidence to high confidence in short order.

Eye Contact

The habit of poor eye contact, or no eye contact, is one of the biggest obstacles people face. A speaker must connect eye to eye with the listener because without that connection, the listener will interpret it as fear. They won't trust the speaker. Trust is a crucial element in communication. Furthermore, without

High Confidence	Low Confidence
Keeping body still	Fidgeting
Being precise	Mumbling
Maintaining good posture	Slouching
Taking space	Talking too fast
Using concise wording	Looking away
Moving with certainty	Using qualifiers
Keeping head still when speaking	Touching face
Making gestures strong and firm	Scratching
Using downward inflections to end sentences	Using upward inflections

eye contact, the speaker loses much of the information being delivered back from the listener. This ineffective communication can waste valuable time.

One way to get past the nerves of fear is to practice maintaining eye contact while presenting. I suggest my clients count in their heads "one two three" while looking directly at a person in the audience. Sometimes I'll point to the audience person I want my client to look at, or I'll walk behind a different audience member and point to the top of their head, guiding my student to look at the person in a back row—and count "one two three."

If the "one two three" technique doesn't work and the speaker is still not calming down enough to practice eye contact, I'll suggest they speak a short phrase while making eye contact with an audience member. The speaker might say for instance, "Here are the numbers." while looking an audience member easily in the eyes. Then moving on to another person with the next short phrase.

The critical part of this exercise, like many exercises I suggest, is feeling it and practice. Getting better at making eye contact needs practice. Once a student feels the rhythm while looking at people in the eyes, they recognize all the feedback they're receiving from the listener, allowing a productive exchange to happen in the present moment.

I've often noticed when a speaker is looking at a particular person and giving them attention, other audience members want to be acknowledged too. We seem to act like seven year olds! "Look at me! Look at me!" The audience starts paying more attention in hopes the speaker will look at them as well.

I can say the effect on audiences is remarkable. I've seen people sit up straighter, or lean forward, or pay closer attention because they want the presenter to acknowledge their attentive listening. I don't know the why of it, only the resulting behavior.

Being in the present moment, speaking eye to eye with another person or with an entire group works! It is fundamental to having effective communication. Audiences become much more animated, excited, and engaged when the speaker makes the listener feel personally involved in the communication process.

Controlling the Room

When it comes to high-powered, highly educated, goal-oriented achievers, controlling the room is critical. When I get a speaker to understand and *feel* they're in the status position, we practice a few techniques. They become much more dynamic. And, it's more fun!

All too frequently during presentations, there's a person in the room who wants to steal the limelight by asking too many questions or starting an off-topic discussion. Here are some techniques to manage that type of person without offense or argument.

Taking Back the Stage

The Challenger

Step 1: Turn the challenge into a question.

Step 2: Rephrase the challenge neutrally. Breathe.

Step 3: Respond using neutral tones and "smiling" eyes.

Step 4: Supply evidence rather than your opinion.

Step 5: Respond to the whole group and finish looking at someone else.

Handling Side Conversations

Step 1: Wait to see if they finish up quickly.

Step 2: Continue what you are saying.

Step 3: Slowly walk toward the "talkers" while looking at others.

Step 4: Move toward them until they stop speaking.

Step 5: Give them positive eye contact as soon as they stop speaking.

Step 6: Slowly walk back to the front of the room.

In private coaching sessions and workshops, I practice dealing with "the challenger" or with handling side conversations through role-playing. I ask for a volunteer or assign one person as the speaker and another to be the challenger. I instruct the speaker how to work through the process of taking back the stage and reassert control over the room. It's a learned and practiced technique, not something that is intuitive to a presenter when they find themselves being challenged. Even comedians need to learn how to manage hecklers.

When necessary to help a speaker, I may ask a couple of students to start a distracting side conversation, allowing the speaker to roleplay handling that situation. The beauty of role playing is that our physical body can't tell whether the experience is real or not. The body reacts in its truth of the experience. When the body has rehearsed the helpful behavior, it will remember the techniques, so when improvisation techniques are experienced, they become internalized. Any trained speaker will feel when they're in the old habitual pattern of obstruction and when they're in the new powerful way of presenting.

Commanding a room happens in phases. The first phase is to stand looking at the audience, and taking stage with quiet confidence as outlined above. Most of the time, that's enough to quiet the room.

But what do you do when a large audience won't stop talking? I'll share a technique I've borrowed from the auctioneer Keith McLane, who runs the largest charity benefit auction company on the west coast. Keith has successfully used this technique at hundreds of events.

When people don't stop talking, Keith says to the room, "Ladies and gentlemen, I want you to do me a favor. If someone to your right is talking, I want you to look at them and say 'shhhh.'" (He'll hold up a finger to his mouth to demonstrate.) "If someone to your left is talking, I want you to look at them and say 'shhhh.'"

The beauty of this technique is that the audience shushes itself! Contrast that with you, as the presenter, interrupting yourself to ask people to be quiet. Even though you might be justified, you become less likable. Peer pressure is far more effective.

Gestures

Actors call it "clown hands." When we're not in the moment, and we're not clear on our intention, and we're being self-conscious and focused on ourselves, and everybody's looking at us, all of a sudden, we're worried about "where do I put my hands?"

It seems like we have "clown hands" wearing big white gloves! I promise you, if you're not committed to your intention and not focused on helping the audience when you deliver your presentation, you're going to be self-conscious and guess what—you won't know what to do with your hands!

One of the things I do to help clients is to teach them to begin by standing in a neutral position. Simply stand, breathe, let hands and arms hang, then begin the presentation. Miraculously, your hands will move. They'll automatically point or gesture—they'll take care of themselves and do their job.

If that doesn't work, and the speaker is still tight, I suggest the presenter speak about a subject they know very well for a minute or so. It can be about their pet dog. I instruct them to *overemphasize* their gestures. If they're communicating negative information, they might give a strong "thumbs down" or if it's a positive comment they can do a big "thumbs up." If the presenter is indicating a location, I will have them point east or west, or counting 1 2 3 4 using their fingers. The speaker needs the ability to use their hands and appropriate gestures to help the audience see and understand their message.

Impromptu Q&A

This is a favorite obstacle among participants! I ask "Who likes impromptu questions?" Most students tell me they hate them and they don't like being put on the spot. Some don't mind getting interrupted with questions, but generally, people find it off-putting.

One of two things will occur when an inexperienced speaker is asked impromptu questions.

They will automatically start talking, and continue to talk and talk too much. There will be countless "ands," "sos," and "buts" added to their responses well beyond what the audience can suffer. The other response leaves a presenter speechless, a deer in the proverbial headlights, while their brain seemingly implodes.

I offer a format for responding to impromptu questions that help speakers think before they respond.

Thank the questioner for the question, but no need to thank them each time. This thank you is polite and will become a mental "time and place holder" in the future, when you need to take the time to select the format or pattern for your response.

Step 1: THINK
I instruct the speaker to select one of three patterns of organization.

- past, present, future
- reasons one, two, three
- pros and cons

Step 2: THEN SPEAK

Make an introductory remark, often by thanking the questioner for the question. "Thank you, Bob. I'm happy to speak on. . . " Doing so allows the brain time to focus on your response. As stated above, you don't need to say "thank you" for every question every single time, but when the first question is asked, it's a good idea.

To practice this technique requires focused coaching. At first attempt, the participant will forget to select a response pattern and start answering the question, talking away. I usually ask them which format they were using and they realize they hadn't selected one! There's often laughter because we could tell they had no format. We begin the exercise again with a new question. They get the technique and learn the difference.

I developed a list of impromptu questions for different occupations and scenarios. There is a different series of practice impromptu questions for executives who might be asked something awkward at a board meeting, or for engineers who have to answer a technical question, or for salespeople who are faced with a difficult prospect. The impromptu questions they'll ultimately face might be different, but the process can be learned and practiced.

When speakers practice fielding impromptu questions, they begin to understand and experience the reality that there is more time available than their racing brains comprehend. They are then able to take their time answering. They have time to come up with calm responses and use valuable pauses. The audience will sense the confidence and wait! Thanking the questioner, and making a conscious decision to use one of three simple response patterns, makes it easier to formulate an impromptu response that is organized, clear, and precise.

Responding in a format makes listening easier for the audience. For instance, if you say, "There are three reasons why we should relocate the office," and you start to list them, the audience will sense the pattern and will follow you. The audience will relax and become more attentive when they view the speaker as a leader who's in the driver's seat.

The obstacles described in this chapter will get in the way of your effectiveness. Letting go of your old habits and replacing them with these helpful techniques will allow you to craft your own style and express it. What makes you unique and special won't be covered over by those no-longer-useful negative habits. Audiences want to see your authentic expression, and by replacing old patterns of behavior with proven techniques, your communications will shine and will touch listeners.

I often think of each new student as a block of gorgeous marble. I see the polished presenter deep inside. The techniques I use and offer are there to help people discover the natural talent hidden inside. Chipping away at a speaker's obstacles ultimately reveals an honest and powerful presenter. It's an honor for me to witness the positive shifts and transformations in clients and observe real communication taking place.

Chapter 12

Collaboration

"You need to be aware of what others are doing, applaud their efforts, acknowledge their successes, and encourage them in their pursuits. When we all help one another, everybody wins."

Jim Stovall

COLLABORATING IN GROUPS

On the second day of the workshop, I introduce students to a collaborative experience through an improvisation exercise I've used throughout my coaching career. It's called The Magic Machine.

The Magic Machine is designed to foster collaboration within groups of individuals by having participants focus on a group activity with a commitment to concentration and teamwork. The goal of this exercise is to build a "human machine" in which participants are engaged in intentional cooperation. There's no lecture about collaboration. Instead, this exercise is designed for students to work together as a unit and quickly experience the payoff of collaboration. Through building this human machine, participants collaborate on a physical and emotional level. Most importantly—It's fun!

Here's how the Magic Machine works.

I give specific instructions about what is going to take place, then ask for a volunteer. The volunteer stands in our "play area" and is instructed to create and perform a unique sound with a corresponding movement.

The sound and the movement shouldn't be overly aerobic (like jogging in place) since this activity continues throughout the exercise. I might suggest an easy sound with a simple, rhythmic movement, like waving an arm up and down while saying, "Aha!" Once our volunteer begins the process, they continue, under my instructions, as the exercise evolves.

Nine times out of ten, the volunteer starts smiling or giggling because they're uncomfortable and feeling self-conscious, acting "silly" in front of their colleagues. Laughter is often a natural response to deflect anxiety.

I tell my students, "Don't question the exercise method yet. If you don't trust yourselves and if you resist the momentum of the exercise, it won't work."

A second participant goes into the play area and physically attaches themselves to the volunteer by, say, putting a hand on a shoulder. The second participant adds their unique sound, coordinating their movement with the volunteer who is still waving an arm saying "Aha!" One by one, each team member enters and attaches themselves to the machine.

We're building a human machine where students intentionally coordinate their sounds and movements rhythmically together. Some students will often feel silly and begin smiling or laughing too, because now colleagues are touching, maybe on a knee, or on top of a head. Embarrassment can set in. I remind my students to commit and concentrate on being the machine. Machines have no emotions or sense of humor.

As each new person joins in, the machine keeps expanding. After all the course participants are linked together, we have fourteen to sixteen people physically connected while making different, coordinated rhythmic sounds and movements.

When everyone is connected and fully committed to concentrating, without smiling, laughing, or losing concentration, the group reaches "machine status," expressing no emotion—simply doing the job of the machine they created.

I explain that I will clap to speed the machine up or slow the machine down, like an orchestra conductor. Students gradually lose their inhibitions and feel energized by the experience. They have become a human machine.

To complete the exercise, I slow the machine participants down until there is no more movement, only silence. The class spontaneously erupts into applause, congratulating each other.

"I enjoyed your sound, and the rhythm was fantastic!" "Your movement was so original!"

They have experienced collaboration. Out of their collective imaginations, they created something that hadn't existed before. And it feels fantastic.

The Magic Machine creates strong bonds and camaraderie like no lecture I could deliver. It is why I don't use valuable workshop time talking about collaboration. The Magic Machine is far more effective. It demonstrates the power found in working in tandem with others. Students always become closer to each other and noticeably more supportive throughout the workshop.

Students are more open and generous with each other after this experience. In class, they may not immediately associate why they feel closer; they simply have fun working side by side. Individuals become more confident and open to giving others support and compliments when engaging in adventurous activities. Supporting one another is one secret weapon for building lasting confidence.

Giving Feedback

Collaboration rarely happens in groups unless participants can give each other candid feedback. Throughout my teaching career, I've learned that there are productive and not-so-productive ways to give feedback and that using proper technique is critical to getting positive outcomes.

Before participants engage in giving feedback to each other, I explain that as the communications professional, at first I'm the most qualified to critique and to offer "adjustments" to students making workshop presentations. It's helpful for the group to observe the established feedback process and understand why it must be followed.

Up until the Magic Machine exercise, participants in the program are not allowed to state an opinion about their classmates' performance. They have opinions—I can tell—because they respond spontaneously to humor or appear disengaged, etc. But now they have experienced and observed more specific presentation skills techniques. They are a more discerning audience.

After a student group is firmly bonded and genuinely supportive of one another, we move on to the next phase of training. I instruct participants on how to deliver suggestions for their peers' improvement. Participants are now invited to make comments about each other's performances and offer feedback, following a set of guidelines.

I learned to give feedback from professional directors giving adjustments to their actors during a rehearsal, and I teach it that way. In the industry, it is known as "giving notes." The process I follow is suggested by the acclaimed director and founder of San Francisco's American Conservatory Theater, William Ball, in his book *A Sense of Direction*.

- First, you state the positive up front. You might say, "Your intention was clear as you entered the restaurant." Nurturing directors proceed with the positive first. In an acting rehearsal, a director may give actors copious notes on things the actor needs to address. All those notes are digested more easily if the actor can latch on to a positive comment first.

- After acknowledging the positive, you offer your thoughts on what adjustments will *add value*. For example: "Pick up your cue after the waiter welcomes you."

- Suggestions must always be delivered with intentional kindness, especially any feedback that might be construed as unflattering or ego deflating.

After the speaker has presented and I've delivered my critical assessment, I ask the presenter if they are open to receiving feedback from their fellow group members. It is always the student's choice, and their choice is to be respected. I don't recall ever hearing, "No, I don't want feedback."

Through this process, participants learn how to give and accept collaborative feedback while working within and in front of groups.

Here is the last, and perhaps most important aspect of the process. The presenter is not allowed to engage in any back and forth responses during their feedback session. The presenter may be bursting to engage in a dialogue, but they are restricted to only saying, "Thank you."

Why is that important? At this point, it is counterproductive to say more.

I know when presenters are given leeway to respond, their minds are busy racing to prepare a response or an explanation instead of listening intently. Limiting the reply to "thank you," students have the opportunity to focus on listening to *all* of the feedback. This eliminates arguing and creates the best chance of absorbing a higher percentage of critical feedback without deflecting or defending.

Actors collaborate this way, allowing artistic expressions to deepen while adhering to set boundaries. Hearing collaborative feedback while being fully present is priceless. This practice is helpful in a business setting, too, because this feedback system fosters essential mutual respect and kindness. Your company may practice different methods of delivering feedback or bad news in management, one-on-one situations. My suggestion is to apply whichever method works best to encourage improvement and a successful outcome.

After a recent workshop attended by sixteen senior managers of a New York-based tech company, I received a follow-up text communication from their hardware engineer program manager. It was the day of their high-stakes developer's conference, and she said:

"We're at the conference now, and they're knocking them dead! They got together and did the breathing exercise you taught in the workshop. They're supporting each other— Thank you!!" That's collaborative teamwork.

Remember, collaboration is something my students learn by doing and experiencing, incorporating all the pieces of presentation influence they gain in my seminars and training programs. It is an intentional byproduct of all the training in groups we do, not a separate syllabus topic.

In my experience, the most powerful way to encourage a collaborative team is to have them face their presentation fears together, in the present moment, while supporting each other in practicing the techniques to relieve their stress, guide them through the Magic Machine improvisation exercise, and then give them the tools to provide each other with helpful feedback.

So while it is not a separate part of any of my training programs, collaboration truly is the main point in learning and implementing all the techniques I teach in classes and have outlined in this book. I am gratified that my workshop participants consistently tell me that they are equipped to communicate much more effectively, which often translates into greater influence, happier customers, and better relationships of all kinds.

AFTERWORD

What is my intention? For the past twenty years, I've been using the honest and straightforward methodology described in this book to help speakers through the knothole of fear. My intention is to help people discover their individual potential and, in that process, transform themselves from average speakers into powerful presenters with unlimited opportunities to captivate and influence others.

This book distills the knowledge and experience I have gained through trial and error over a lifetime as an actor, coach, teacher, and trainer. When I came up with ideas that worked, I used and refined them. Others I borrowed, adapted, and developed into new techniques for my training programs.

In sum, the keys to presentation excellence are an understanding and practice of present-moment awareness using acting techniques, which include these four foundational principles.

Body: How the body and your awareness of the present moment play vital roles in all of your presentations and communications.

Voice: How to use your voice as an instrument to achieve better diction, enunciation, projection, and voice modulation, to more effectively communicate your story.

Intention: How a specific intention and connecting that intention to a strong feeling aids in the manageability of fear, nerves, and self-consciousness when presenting to an audience.

Improvisation: How improvisation allows you to release your instinctive creativity and learn by doing.

Everyone is afraid to speak in public at some point. My goal is to help fearful or nervous speakers to *say it anyway*!

Please take the ideas outlined in this book and apply them. They will hold you in good stead. The more you practice, the more confident you will be.

There is no limit to how influential a presenter you can become; the only limitation you face is yourself. You can do this!

"Now. Breathe. In. . . and out. In. . . and out. In. . . and out."

About the Author

Billie is the Founder of Billie Shepard & Associates and has been a presentation coach as well as a professional actor, acting coach, and speaker for decades. She facilitates workshops that train corporate executives, HR professionals, engineers, financial analysts, managers, and public speakers from all over the world to be better presenters, leaders, collaborators, and communicators. Among her clients are Uber, Cisco Systems, Intuit, Splunk, Rackspace, Thumbtack, Lockheed Martin, Seiler LLP, Wells Fargo, Bayer, Dermira, University of California Santa Cruz Silicon Valley Extension, University of California Berkeley Extension, International Humphrey Fellowship participants, and thousands of professional actors.

She has been a guest speaker and coach at conferences, seminars, and universities including Harvard Alumni Association, Stanford University, San Jose State University, San Jose-Silicon Valley Chamber of Commerce, UC Berkeley Extension, and UCSC Silicon Valley Extension. She was the founder and coordinator of the Women in Business Institute at UCSC Extension.

Billie founded two acting academies and five acting workshops in four states. Among these is the Actors Workshop at San Jose Repertory Theatre, Directing Yourself at Voice One Studios in San Francisco, and The Monologue Workshop at San Francisco's Full Circle Productions. She has produced and hosted workshops including such notable guest instructors as Academy Award winner Alan Arkin and Michael Kostroff, costar on The Wire. Both have written about her influence in their books.

Billie has appeared in lead roles in regional theatre productions in California, Texas, and Arizona. She has been featured in TV productions such as Nash Bridges as well as many national commercials, including Curel Lotion and Camay.

A Dean's Scholar with a Bachelor of Arts in Creative Arts and a Masters in Theatre Arts from San Jose State University, Billie published her Master's thesis on the application of acting techniques in business presentations entitled *The Actor Within: An Exploration of Present-Moment Awareness in Business Presentations*. *The Billie Shepard Presentation Method* is a culmination of her acting and teaching careers and her extensive educational research.

> *If you're interested in bringing Billie to your company to conduct her workshop, or for individual coaching, she can be reached at her website **www.billieshepard.com** or directly at **billie@billieshepard.com**.*

Index

Note: Page numbers in italics refer to illustrative material.

Made in the USA
Monee, IL
06 May 2023

32942067R00094